Words

John Seely is a writer and editor of books about language and communication. He is an experienced teacher and has been a full-time author for many years. He is Series Editor of the *One Step Ahead* books, and author of *The Oxford Guide to Writing and Speaking* and *Everyday Grammar*.

One Step Ahead ...

The *One Step Ahead* series is for all those who want and need to communicate more effectively in a range of real-life situations. Each title provides up-to-date practical guidance, tips, and the language tools to enhance your writing and speaking.

Series Editor: John Seely

Titles in the series

Editing and Revising Text	Jo Billingham
Essays and Dissertations	Chris Mounsey
Organizing and Participating in Meetings	Judith Leigh
Publicity, Newsletters, and Press Releases	Alison Baverstock
Punctuation	Robert Allen
Spelling	Robert Allen
Words	John Seely
Writing for the Internet	Jane Dorner
Writing Reports	John Seely

Acknowledgements

I should like to thank the staff at Oxford University Press, especially Alysoun Owen and Helen Cox for their help and support in the production of this book. I also thank my wife, Elizabeth for her suggestions, comments, and support during the period when it was being written.

Words

John Seely

Cartoons by Beatrice Baumgartner-Cohen

OXFORD UNIVERSITY PRESS

Great Clarendon Street, Oxford OX2 6DP

Oxford University Press is a department of the University of Oxford.
It furthers the University's objective of excellence in research, scholarship,
and education by publishing worldwide in
Oxford New York
Auckland Bangkok Buenos Aires Cape Town Chennai
Dar es Salaam Delhi Hong Kong Istanbul Karachi Kolkata
Kuala Lumpur Madrid Melbourne Mexico City Mumbai Nairobi
São Paulo Shanghai Singapore Taipei Tokyo Toronto

Oxford is a registered trade mark of Oxford University Press
in the UK and in certain other countries

Published in the United States
by Oxford University Press Inc., New York

British Library Cataloguing in Publication Data
Data available

Library of Congress Cataloging in Publication Data
Data available

ISBN 0-19-866282-3

10 9 8 7 6 5 4 3 2

Design and typesetting by David Seabourne
Printed in Spain by Book Print S.L.

Contents

1 | Introduction

'I am a bear of very little brain and long words bother me', said A. A. Milne's Winnie the Pooh. There are occasions when many of us share Pooh's feelings about our capacity to cope with words. The sheer volume of new words that seem to flood into the language every day is daunting. On the Internet there are whole websites devoted to new words. Some even offer to deliver a new word by email every day. And what words! Could you, for example, put a meaning to *geocaching, evangineer, plutography,* or *velcroid*? If the answer is 'no'—well, neither could I until I started writing this book.

It's almost certain you could manage pretty well without those four words (although I must confess to a sneaking attachment to *velcroid*) and the thousands of others that are coined each year. On the other hand, many people feel that they would like some help in coping with the words that already exist and are well established in the language. It is to these readers that this book is addressed.

So what *One Step Ahead: Words* offers is a comprehensive strategy to tackling vocabulary. The book is divided into two parts:

Part A

This part of the book outlines a strategy for tackling vocabulary and provides information on a wide range of topics:

Chapter 2: How many words do you know?
An overview of what we mean by a person's 'vocabulary', and how we can set about selecting the best word for a particular situation.

Chapter 3: Looking words up
How to choose and use dictionaries, thesauruses and other word books.

Chapter 4: Effective communication
Assessing the level of your audience and choosing the best words for clear communication.

Chapter 5: When the words get in the way
Adjusting your vocabulary to fit the social situation in which you are communicating. Taboo, euphemisms, slang and jargon.

Chapter 6: Where do English words come from?
A brief survey of the history of English showing the influences of different languages and cultures over the years.

Chapter 7: Newspeak
New words today—where they come from and why they are coined.

Chapter 8: The grammar of words
A brief and simple introduction to some of the grammatical words you need to be able to talk about words: noun, adjective, verb, adverb. How words are built up: stem, prefix, suffix.

Chapter 9: Getting a grip on words
An overview of the strategy.

Part B: Reference section

▓ Word classes
More about the grammar of words.

▓ Prefixes
A list of the commonest prefixes with meanings and examples.

▓ Suffixes
How we use suffixes to make new words.

▓ Confusables
A list of the words most commonly confused with explanations of their meaning and sample sentences.

▓ Glossary
Explanations of the technical terms used in this book.

▓ Resources
Useful word books and websites.

2 How many words do you know?

Building your vocabulary

People are sometimes judged by their vocabulary: 'He's very well educated; he uses a lot of long words.' Some feel challenged because they feel that their own personal vocabulary is not adequate for the job they have to do. A popular feature of *Reader's Digest* for many years was 'It Pays to Increase Your Wordpower'. The idea that knowing a lot of words gives you some kind of 'power' is widespread.

But what does it mean? How many words do you know? It is sometimes suggested that you can measure this by a simple test:

Take a dictionary that has between 1500 and 2500 words.

Select at random 1% of the pages, spreading your selection throughout the book.

Count the number of words you know on each of the pages you have chosen.

Multiply the total by 100. The result is the number of words you know.

It sounds easy. In fact as soon as you try it, you come up against two major problems:

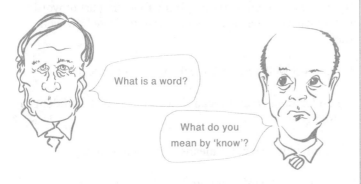

What is a word?

What do you mean by 'know'?

What is a word?

If you go through a page of a dictionary in the way suggested you soon find yourself having to make decisions about which words to count and which to ignore. Take the word 'lament' for example. It has two uses:

■ as a verb, meaning to express sadness, grief or regret;

■ as a noun, meaning an expression of sadness, grief or regret.

Verbs, nouns, and adjectives are explained in Chapter 8, and in the Glossary

Do you count that as two words or one? And what about:

'lamented' (adjective)?

'lamenting' (adjective)?

Then there are words that are clearly related to 'lament':

'lamentation'

'lamentable'

Anyone who knows 'lament' can reasonably claim to know these too. So for that one 'word' you could claim to know anything between one (rather strict) and six (rather generous) 'words'.

What do we mean by 'know'?

Try this experiment. Go through the following list of words and for each one write down a letter to indicate how well you know it:

A I know it well and would feel confident to use it.

B I understand what it means but wouldn't feel confident to use it.

C I think I know what it means, but I'm not sure.

D I've seen or heard it but don't really know what it means.

E I don't think I've ever seen it before in my life.

denizen	denounce	dentate	denunciation
denn	dense	denticulate	denutrition
dennet	densify	dentist	deny
denomination	dent	denuclearize	deobstruct
denote	dental	denumbiate	deodar

As you can see from this exercise we 'know' different words in different ways. (And if you put anything except 'E' against 'denumbiate' you were cheating because I made it up!)

Passive or active?

Probably the most important distinction to make is between our active and passive vocabularies. The active vocabulary (Group A) is the list of words that we feel confident about using. The passive vocabulary (Group B) contains the words we are fairly sure we understand but which we don't really feel confident to use ourselves. Naturally your passive vocabulary is bigger than your active vocabulary—typically for an adult about 25 per cent bigger. So one way to increase your 'word-power' is to move words from the passive list to the active one:

make sure that you really do know what they mean and how they are used and then start using them!

Secondly, you can begin to take a more active approach to your 'fringe' vocabulary, the words that fall into groups C and D: words that you think you know, but aren't really sure about and words that you recognize but don't know the meaning of. In both cases the solution is simple: make use of a good-quality dictionary.

Thirdly, you can increase the passive and 'fringe' vocabularies by reading more widely. Although magazine quizzes along the lines of 'It Pays to Increase Your Wordpower' tests are fun, they don't really work because the words in them are completely out of context. The words you have gained since leaving formal education have come into your head because you have read or heard them. They no doubt include many words you have acquired for use at work. Reading takes you away from this familiar world and into worlds of language that you might otherwise not encounter. The more serious programmes on radio and TV do the same thing. Again, you need to use a good dictionary to gain the most benefit from your reading, listening, and viewing.

Call My Bluff

A popular TV show for many years involved two teams who took it in turns to test each other's wordpower. A team would be given an unusual word, for example **spauld**. Each member of the team would offer the opposing team a possible and plausible definition of the word. Their opponents then had to guess which one was true:

1 *This is a term from an early form of croquet. To **spauld** was to prevent an opponent's leading ball from finishing by cannoning into it and knocking it out of bounds.*

2 *The term **spauld** comes from the ancient craft of fletching, or putting the feathered flights on arrows. A spauld was a tool used by the fletcher to trim the flights to exactly the right size.*

3 *It's a term from butchery. The **spauld** of an animal is its shoulder. The word later came to mean any joint of meat.*

Answer

The correct answer is 3, 'a joint of meat'.

11

Fitting new words into a pattern

The approach just outlined will work, but it is a bit random. There are probably more than a million words in the English language, and an educated speaker of English may have a total vocabulary of between 25,000 and 75,000 words. (Calculations of Shakespeare's vocabulary usually come in at around 30,000 words.) In the list on page 10 you probably didn't know some of the words for a very good reason: you didn't need to. There is no particular virtue in piling up in your head words that you are never going to need to use. What you need is a system. You need to be able to fit each new word into a pattern which helps you understand:

- its grammar;

- its structure and origins;

- how it relates to other words with similar meanings;

- how it combines with other words;

- the situations in which it is used.

*Zounds!
I was never so
bethumped
with words since
I first called my
father dad.*

King John

Grammar

It should go without saying that a new word is of little value if you don't know how to use it in a sentence. Knowing the class or classes that a word belongs to is therefore essential. It is also, sometimes, a handy way of extending your vocabulary. Many words belong to more than one class, but you may well find that you are unconsciously limiting your vocabulary by ignoring this fact. You may, for example, be accustomed to using 'articulate' as an adjective:

She was a very **articulate** supporter of women's rights.

but never as a verb:

She was trying to **articulate** the different ways in which women had been oppressed over the centuries.

*When they call
you **articulate**
that's another
way of saying
'He talks good for
a black guy'.*

Ice-T, American rap musician

Structure

Some words have a simple construction: they consist of only one part and cannot be broken down further. For example:

string money pepper gossip buggy

Others can be broken down into a number of constituent parts. For example:

complication = com + plic + ate

explicable = ex + plic + able

extricate = ex + tric + ate

If you understand what prefixes such as 'com-' and 'ex-', and suffixes such as '-able' and '-ate' contribute to the meaning and usage of a word, you have a powerful tool for understanding new words and extending your vocabulary.

Roots

In a similar way, it is helpful to be on the lookout for words that have common roots. There is a mass of English words that have been built up on words (or parts of words) from classical Greek and Latin. Even if you have no knowledge of these languages yourself, it shouldn't take long to work out what the original word or part of a word must have been and roughly what it meant. All these words, for example, have a common ancestor:

biography biology bionic bio-diversity biosphere

Clearly words containing 'bio' have something do with life. Similarly 'auto**graph**', 'mono**graph**', and '**graph**ology' suggest that words containing 'graph' have to do with writing. So putting 'bio' and 'graph' together in 'biography' gives us 'writing about life'. A good dictionary will provide further information about such word derivations.

bionic
■ adj.
1 relating to or denoting the use of electro-mechanical body parts instead of or as well as living ones.
2 informal having ordinary human powers increased by or as if by the aid of such devices.

Concise Oxford Dictionary

Grouping words by meaning

Another valuable way of gaining a grasp on the vocabulary of
English is to look for patterns of meaning. Often when we
speak or write, we feel that we have a choice of two or more
words with similar meanings. For example, how many words
can you think of to fill the space in this sentence?

'Please leave me alone,' she _____.

Possibles include:

said	shouted	yelled	cried	screamed
shrieked	whispered	murmured	muttered	mumbled
sighed	gasped	panted	yelped	growled
snapped	snarled	squeaked	whined	sobbed
wailed	drawled			

Linguists call such groups of words 'semantic fields', since
semantics is the study of meaning. The easiest place to find
such groupings in a practical, usable form is a thesaurus. If you
are stuck for the exact word for a particular shade of meaning,
then a thesaurus is a valuable tool. One has to beware, however. Successful use of a thesaurus depends on two things:

■ You have to know the exact meanings of the words it lists, or
  be prepared to research their meanings.

■ You have to know exactly how they are used.

Clearly, some of the words in the list above either would be
inappropriate or would take a little explaining. Think, for
example, of situations in which you might say or write:

'Please leave me alone,' she snarled.

or

'Please leave me alone,' she drawled.

or

'Please leave me alone,' she growled.

How precise do you want to be?

So far we have looked at choosing between words with different shades of meaning. 'Shout', 'scream', and 'yell' have similar meanings but they are not the same. We will choose one of them depending on the volume, pitch, and emotional content of the sound we are trying to describe. You normally expect a scream, for example, to be higher-pitched than a shout and possibly louder. It certainly implies that the person doing it is expressing stronger emotion.

There is another kind of choice: that of precision. Consider the following sentence:

She is a very keen gardener and when I last saw her she was planting out some _____.

There is a large number of words we could use to fill this space. For example:

alpines	annuals	begonias	bulbs
daffodils	daisies	flowers	gentians
pansies	perennials	petunias	saxifrages
tulips			

Which to choose? The answer might be: 'The right one to describe whatever she was planting.' While that would narrow the field, it would not provide a final answer. Suppose she was planting saxifrages; then we could use 'saxifrages', or 'alpines', or 'flowers'. We could even say 'saxifraga aizoides' or 'saxifraga burseriana'. The word(s) we choose will depend on how precise we want to be, and that in turn will depend on our audience and our purpose in addressing them. It is a question of precision.

Hierarchies of words

All the words in the list can be placed in a hierarchy:

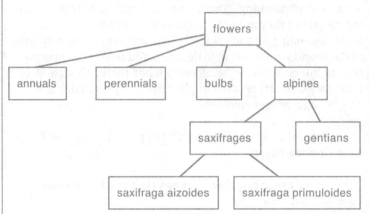

As you move down the branches of the hierarchy the words become more and more precise. (And the likelihood of people knowing and understanding them decreases.)

Such hierarchies of words (or groups of **hyponyms**, as linguists term them) are also part of our way of thinking. When we speak or write we choose a word at the right level for our purposes. If we are stuck for precisely the right word then we often have to go up a level and use a more general word than we would like—and find other ways of communicating our meaning:

The company words keep

Words don't, of course, exist in isolation. We combine them with other words into phrases and sentences. Certain words typically occur in combination with other words.

All the words in the list that follows have related meanings:

belief	opinion	view	position	attitude
feeling	notion	idea	impression	suspicion

Suppose that we want to put them into a sentence that begins like this:

She _____ the
| belief that ... |
| opinion |
| view | that ...
| *etc.* |

Which verb should we use to fill the blank? Normally you would expect either 'had' or 'held'. Can we use each of these words for all the words in the list? And are there other words we can use? Most of the time we carry these word combinations in our heads. Years of reading and listening have 'programmed' our brains to expect them. When we encounter a word for the first time, it is not so easy. Some dictionaries provide examples of usage:

---

suspicion
1 Suspicion is the feeling that you do not trust someone or that something is wrong in some way, although you have no evidence for this. EG Derek had always shared Lynn's suspicion of Michael ... I had aroused his suspicions last week ... Their friendship is regarded with suspicion by their teachers.

Collins Cobuild English Language Dictionary

---

*Suspicions
among thoughts
are like bats
among birds,
they ever fly
by twilight.*

Francis Bacon

Situation, situation, situation

There is yet one more way of sorting words: according to the social situation in which you might use them. If you look at a typical entry in a thesaurus you can see that not all the words it contains are suitable for all social situations:

false accusation, false charge, false evidence, fake confession, perjured testimony, perjury...calumny, scandal, defamation...plant (Inf), cooked-up charge (Inf), put-up job (Inf), put-up (Inf), frame-up (Inf), frame (Inf)

Bloomsbury Thesaurus

Clearly the situation where you would use the word 'calumny' is very different from that where you might refer to a 'frame-up'.

In dictionaries and other books about words you will encounter these descriptions of words:

▨ formal

This refers to vocabulary that can always be used with a wide range of audiences, including people whom you don't know. Its use will hardly ever offend, but may sound a little 'starchy' in informal situations.

▨ informal, colloquial

These words and phrases may not be suitable for use with some audiences and some may even be offended by their use. It is advisable to avoid them if you don't know your audience well enough to judge their likely response.

▨ slang

Very informal language containing a number of specialist words. Slang is very often peculiar to one particular social group. So there is schoolboy slang and computer slang, for example.

▨ taboo

This is a sociological term and refers to words and expressions that part or all of a society has 'outlawed'. In British English this group includes words referring to sexual activities and parts of the body. As social attitudes change, words may move from being taboo into the area of slang and informal language. It is also possible for words that were once acceptable in certain social groupings to become taboo.

To sum up ...

1. Your vocabulary is the words that you know. These can be active (the words you are happy to use in speech and writing) or passive (the words that you understand when you hear or read them but are not yet confident about using yourself).

2. You can increase your active vocabulary by increasing your passive vocabulary and by moving words from your passive to your active vocabulary.

3. Add words to your passive vocabulary by being aware of new words when you come across them and by making sure that you know what they mean.

4. Make passive words active by deliberately setting out to use them—but first make sure that you are confident you know what they mean and how they are used (and how to pronounce them).

5. You should fit all new words into a pattern. This includes knowing about their grammar and usage.

6. Learn what grammatical class a word belongs to.

7. Link it to other words in the same family.

8. Find out its precise meaning and when to use it in preference to another word with a similar meaning.

9. Check that you know which other words it normally combines with.

10. Be aware of the social situations in which particular words may and may not be used.

3 | Looking words up

Introduction

If you wish to improve and extend your active vocabulary, it is essential to be able to look words up. Good reference books will enable you to:

■ discover the exact meaning of a word;

■ find a range of possible words for a particular situation;

■ learn about the usage of particular words;

and much more besides.

In this chapter word books are divided into four groups:

■ dictionaries;

■ thesauruses;

■ usage guides;

■ other word books.

Dictionaries

It's obvious that if you want to find out the meaning of a word you need to look it up in a dictionary. But which dictionary? The choice is overwhelming:

Too large?

The very biggest dictionaries, such as the *Oxford English Dictionary*, contain a wealth of information. This, for example, is the beginning of the entry for the word 'hope':

---

hope (həʊp), *v.* Forms: see HOPE *sb.*[1] [OE. *hopian*, ME. *hopien*, *hopen*, corresp. to MLG., MDu., Du. *hopen*:—OLG. **hopôn*. Not known in OHG.; in MHG. *hoffen* is rare, and chiefly MG., not the regular word for 'to hope'; like the corresp. sb. the vb. appears to have belonged orig. to the English and Saxon-Frankish domain, and thence to have spread in later times over Germany and Scandinavia.]

1. a. *intr.* To entertain expectation of something desired; to look (mentally) with expectation. Const. †*to*, †*after*, †*of* (obs.), *for*; also with indirect passive.

971 *Blickl. Hom.* 87 We to þinum hidercyme hopodan & hyhtan. *c* **1205** LAY. 17936 Ah ne hope þu to ræde of heom þat liggeð dede. *c* **1290** *S. Eng. Leg.* I. 291/97 Ne hopie ich nouȝt þere-fore. *c* **1400** *Cato's Mor.* 203 in *Cursor M.* App. iv. 1672 Quen þou art atte disese, hope ofter better ese. **1553** EDEN *Treat. Newe Ind.* (Arb.) 39 This nauigation..was not brought to the ende hoped for. **1595** T. BEDINGFELD tr. *Machiavelli's Florentine Hist.* 140 The Earle..shut himselfe vp in Poppi, not hoping of any aide. *c* **1600** *My Ladyis Pulcritud* 26 in *Montgomerie's Poems* (1887) 279 Houping aganis all houp. **1659** B. HARRIS *Parival's Iron Age* 29, I can hope for no support in the equity of my cause. **1726** *Adv. Capt. R. Boyle* 16 Come, hope for the best, said I. **1850** TENNYSON *In Mem.* cxii, Hope could never hope too much, In watching thee from hour to hour. *Mod.* I hoped for better things from him.

If you are a scholar, then this level of detailed information may well be very important. For everyday use, however, it is probably rather more than we require. So you need to choose your dictionary wisely.

Too small?

At the other end of the scale the information contained within a mini-dictionary is necessarily limited:

hop *v.* (hopped, hopping) 1 jump on one foot; (of an animal) jump with all feet together. 2 *informal* make a short journey; move quickly to a new position. ● *n.* a hopping movement; a short journey. □ **on the hop** *informal* unprepared.

hop² *n.* a plant used to flavour beer.

hope *n.* expectation of something desired; something giving grounds for this; something hoped for. ● *v.* feel hope. □ **hopeful** *adj.*

hopefully *adv.* 1 in a hopeful way. 2 it is to be hoped.

■ **Usage** The use of *hopefully* to mean 'it is to be hoped' is widely considered incorrect.

hopeless *adj.* 1 without hope. 2 inadequate, incompetent. □ **hopelessly** *adv.*, **hopelessness** *n.*

hopper *n.* 1 a container with an opening at the base for discharging its contents. 2 one who hops.

hopscotch *n.* a game involving hopping over marked squares.

horde *n.* a large group or crowd.

horizon *n.* 1 the line at which earth and sky appear to meet. 2 the limit of someone's knowledge or interests.

horny *adj.* (hornier, horniest) 1 of or like horn; hardened and calloused. 2 *informal* sexually excited.

horology *n.* the measurement of time; the making of clocks. □ **horologist** *n.*

horoscope *n.* a forecast of events based on the positions of stars.

horrendous *adj.* horrifying. □ **horrendously** *adv.*

horrible *adj.* causing horror; very unpleasant. □ **horribly** *adv.*

horrid *adj.* horrible.

horrific *adj.* horrifying. □ **horrifically** *adv.*

horrify *v.* (horrified, horrifying) arouse horror in.

horror *n.* intense shock and fear or disgust; a terrible event or situation; *informal* a naughty child.

hors d'oeuvre (or dervr) *n.* food served as an appetizer.

horse *n.* 1 a four-legged animal with a mane and tail. 2 a padded structure for vaulting over in a gym. □ **horse around** *informal* fool about.

horseback *n.* □ **on horseback** riding on a horse.

horsebox *n.* a vehicle for trans-

Just right

So the first thing to realize about dictionaries is that the information they can give us depends on the size of the dictionary and the purpose for which it was developed. For normal use at home, a single-volume dictionary of 1000–2000 pages is probably the best choice:

hope ● n. 1 a feeling of expectation and desire. ➤ a person or thing that gives cause for hope. ➤ grounds for hoping. 2 archaic a feeling of trust. ● v. expect and desire. ➤ intend if possible to do something.
– PHRASES **hope against hope** cling to a mere possibility. **not a** (or **some**) **hope** informal no chance at all.
– DERIVATIVES **hoper** n.
– ORIGIN OE *hopa* (n.), *hopian* (v.), of Gmc origin.

What dictionaries can and cannot tell us

It is important to understand that dictionaries are essentially historical documents. They can only tell us about how words were used in the past; they cannot tell us exactly how they are used now, let alone how they will be used in the future. This apparently odd statement is only common sense. Even the most up-to-date dictionary was only up to date at the time of going to press. Language is in a constant state of flux, and in the gap between when the dictionary goes to press and when the reader consults it, things will have moved on. So, for example, at the time of writing as far as I know none of the following new words is to be found in a printed dictionary:

plunderphonics

yottabyte

gaydar

obesogenic

chatterati

And this is as it should be: only a few of the new words that are spawned every week will make it into next year, let alone into the next decade. Dictionaries offer us a snapshot of the state of the language at the time when they were prepared. This is why the dictionary departments of major publishers are constantly bringing out new editions of their dictionaries in an attempt to overcome the ravages of time.

But there is another sense in which dictionaries are historical documents. Modern dictionaries are constructed upon historical principles. They acknowledge that language is not fixed but constantly on the move. Old words die, new words are born, and other words gradually change their meanings. Some words, too, are local and rather rare. A 'hope', for example, can mean a piece of enclosed land, but not many people use the word in this way and nowadays it occurs chiefly in place names such as 'Fownhope'.

So dictionaries can tell us how words have been used in the past and what they meant then. They can tell us which of those

plunderphonics, *noun*

A musical technique that creates a new piece of music by mixing passages from a number of existing songs.

logophilia.com

24

meanings were still current at the time the dictionary was written. The extent to which a dictionary provides the details of this historical information will vary according to its size and style. You can see this by comparing the entries for 'hope' from the *Oxford English Dictionary* and the *Concise Oxford Dictionary*. In the latter the historical information is resticted to the fact that the meaning for 'hope' of 'a feeling of trust' is 'archaic',

Larger dictionaries back up their historical information with:

■ etymology
An explanation of where the word originally came from. This, too, can differ in scope, according to the size of the dictionary.

■ quotations
Examples of real language in which the word is used.

Both of these are to be found in the extract from the *Oxford English Dictionary* on page 22. We learn that the word probably came into Old English from the Germanic language of the Saxons. We also see examples of how it was used by John Wyclif and Alexander Pope, among other writers.

Usage

Some dictionaries also provide examples of how a word is used. For example:

> **hope 1.** If you hope that something is true or hope for something to happen, you want it to be true or to happen and usually believe that it is possible or likely. EG Nothing can be done except to wait, hope, and pray ... She hoped she wasn't going to cry ...
>
> **Collins Cobuild English Language Dictionary**

This approach to defining a word is most useful for those learn-ing a language, especially foreign learners of English. It is also useful when you want to move a word from your passive to your active vocabulary.

The information provided by a dictionary

hope n. **1** a feeling of expectation and desire. ➤ a person or thing that gives cause for hope. ➤ grounds for hoping. **2** archaic a feeling of trust. ● v. expect and desire. ➤ intend if possible to do something.
– PHRASES **hope against hope** cling to a mere possibility. **not a** (or **some**) **hope** informal no chance at all.
– DERIVATIVES **hoper** n.
– ORIGIN OE *hopa* (n.), *hopian* (v.), of Gmc origin.

hope chest ● n. N. Amer. a chest in which household linen is stored by a woman in preparation for marriage.

hopeful ● adj. feeling or inspiring hope. ● n. a person likely or hoping to succeed.
– DERIVATIVES **hopefulness** n.

hopefully ● adv. **1** in a hopeful manner. **2** it is to be hoped that: *hopefully it should be finished by next year.*

> USAGE **hopefully**
>
> The traditional sense of **hopefully**, 'in a hopeful manner', has been used since the 17th century. In the 20th century a new use arose, with the meaning 'it is to be hoped that'. This sense is regarded by some traditionalists as incorrect, despite the fact that it is now the dominant use, accounting for more than 90 per cent of citations for hopefully in the British National Corpus.

hopeless ● adj. **1** feeling or causing despair. **2** inadequate; incompetent.
– DERIVATIVES **hopelessly** adv. **hopelessness** n.

hophead ● n. informal **1** US a drug addict. **2** Austral./NZ a heavy drinker.

Hopi /'həʊpi/ ● n. (pl. same or **Hopis**) **1** a member of a Pueblo Indian people living chiefly in NE Arizona. **2** the Uto-Aztecan language of this people.
– ORIGIN the name in Hopi.

hoplite /'hɒplʌɪt/ ● n. a heavily armed foot soldier of ancient Greece.
– ORIGIN from Gk *hoplitēs*, from *hoplon* 'weapon'.

hopper[1] ● n. **1** a container for grain, rock, or rubbish, typically one that tapers downward and discharges its contents at the bottom. ➤ a tapering container, working with a hopping motion, through which grain passes into a mill. **2** a railway wagon able to discharge bulk material through its floor. **3** a barge for carrying away and discharging mud from a dredging-machine. **4** a person or thing that hops. ➤ a hopping insect, especially a young locust.

hopper[2] ● n. a person who picks hops.

headword
The word upon which all this group of dictionary entries and definitions are based. (So the headword 'hope', for example, includes a number of different definitions plus a reference to 'hope chest'.

pronunciation guide
The system used to show how words are pronounced is explained in a set of notes at the beginning of the dictionary.

word class
Usually given in an abbreviated form: 'n' for noun, 'v' for verb, and so on.

derivation
Brief notes on how the word came into the language.

first definition
Many words have more than one meaning or use. These are usually numbered for the sake of clarity.

second definition

usage note
If a particular usage is unusual in some way, this is explained. For example a word may be obsolete ('obs') or informal in use ('inf').

additional information
This can include word combinations (like 'hope chest'), and phrases of expressions using the word (e.g. 'not a hope') .

Using a thesaurus

The name 'thesaurus' comes from a Classical Greek word meaning 'treasury' or 'store', and a thesaurus is just that: a treasure-house of words. The thesaurus was invented in the mid-19th century by Peter Mark Roget who published, in 1852, his *Thesaurus of English Words and Phrases, classified and arranged so as to facilitate the Expression of Ideas and assist in Literary Composition*. Roget organized his work into a number of basic concepts, each of which was then broken down into sub-concepts. Some modern thesauruses follow a modified version of Roget's categories, while others have taken the basic idea and developed in their own way. The *Bloomsbury Thesaurus*, for example, has 23 basic concepts, such as 'Communication'. Each of these is then broken down into sections such as 'Truth' and 'Falsehood'. These are then usually broken down into further sections such as 'authenticity' and within each of these sections words are grouped according to grammatical class (nouns, verbs, adjectives, and adverbs).

The sections of the main part of the thesaurus are numbered with each aspect of a major theme being allocated its own number, for example: **699**. Within each of these sections different aspects of the theme and different word classes (noun, adjective, etc.) are also numbered: **699.1**, **699.2**, and so on. At the end of the many of these subscriptions you will find cross-references to other parts of the thesaurus.

To help you find the word(s) you are looking for there is a substantial index, which refers you to the relevant numbered sections. Typically the index of a thesaurus occupies about one third of the whole book.

Finding what you are looking for in a thesaurus requires a certain amount of skill and commitment. An example is the best way of showing how it works. Suppose you want to describe the coat a woman is wearing and you want to say that it is of fake fur, but you don't much like the word 'fake'.

You begin by looking up the word 'fake' in the index. In the
Bloomsbury Thesaurus, this produces the list in the box below:

> **fake 699.12; 699.37;** 96.12 artificial; 96.7 artificiality;
> 699.25 be fraudulent; 772.11 borrowed; 772.9 borrow
> illegally; 699.19 cheat; 125.2, 125.10 copy; 699.33 deceitful;
> 702.12 deceive; 700.15 deceiver; 699.39 disguised;
> 234.12 distort the truth; 234.8 exaggerated; 699.14 façade;
> 699.36 falsified; 699.26 falsify; 699.35 fraudulent;
> 702.10 hypocritical; 58.3 ice hockey; 772.3, 774.6 illegal
> borrowing; 125 imitation; 700.39 imitative; 699.28 mask;
> 58.9 play hockey; 46.15 play offence
>
> Bloomsbury Thesaurus

It consists of all the occurrences of the word 'fake' in the main
part of the thesaurus. As you can see, they are arranged thematically to help you locate what you are looking for. They also
distinguish between the uses of 'fake' as a noun ('artificiality'),
and adjective ('artificial'), and as a verb ('borrow').

If there is an entry in bold type at the beginning, it is always
best to begin there. In this case there are two, and a quick
check reveals that the first is for nouns (which we don't want)
and the second for adjectives (which we do).

> **699.37**
> **fake,** sham, mock, artificial, imitative, bogus, counterfeit,
> tinselled, rubbishy, junky, phoney (Inf), not all it's cracked up
> to be (Inf)
>
> Bloomsbury Thesaurus

It may be that this first entry will provide what you are
looking for. Certainly 'sham', 'mock', 'artificial', and 'imitative'
(or 'imitation') are possibilities. The Index, however, offers a
number of other lines of enquiry. For example:

> **125.2**
> **copy**, reproduction, image, likeness, replica, model, working
> model, duplication, duplicate, imitation, dummy, mock-up, fac-
> simile, photocopy, picture, portrait, pastiche (or pasticcio), fair
> copy, faithful copy, carbon copy, clone,doppelganger, simula-
> tion, fake, forgery, sham, bootleg, counterfeit, plagiarism,
> disguise, camouflage, crib (Inf), pony (US Inf), rip-off (Inf)
> ➤ 115 Similarity; 561 Reproduction
>
> **Bloomsbury Thesaurus**

This, in turn, suggests a further line of enquiry:

> **115**
> **copy**, photocopy, facsimile (or fax) (copy), stencil, duplicate,
> Mimeograph™, photomechanical transfer (PMT), reproduction,
> imitation, close imitation, pirated record, twin, clone, trend,
> style, fashion, fad, bootleg copy (Inf)
> ➤ 117 Conformity; 553 Fashion
>
> **Bloomsbury Thesaurus**

And the trail could continue further, if you had the time and
the inclination.

The word detective

Usage dictionaries

Guides to usage are frequently arranged alphabetically, and while they are not, strictly speaking, dictionaries, they are such an important supplement to a conventional dictionary that it makes sense to cover them here. Such reference books often announce themselves as usage guides, for example: *Fowler's Modern English Usage* and *The Longman Guide to English Usage*. Others have titles such as *The Good English Guide* and *The Penguin Dictionary of Troublesome Words*.

 Providing advice about usage is a matter of experience, judgement and personal taste, so it is not surprising that different writers give different advice. Here, for example, is what two authors have to say about the use of 'hopefully':

---

hopefully

Besides meaning 'in a hopeful way' (They waited hopefully for the results), this now very commonly means 'it is hoped' (Hopefully they will arrive in time). There is a strong prejudice both in Britain and in the USA against this usage, and the British believe it to be an Americanism. Its users may justify their decision by analogy with adverbs such as naturally, which can mean either 'in a natural way' (His hair curls naturally) or 'it is natural (Naturally I'm coming). The device with **hopefully** is often useful, since one is not obliged to state who is doing the 'hoping'. If you use it, be careful to leave no room for ambiguity between the two possible meanings. They will leave hopefully in the morning might mean either that they will leave with optimism, or that I hope they will succeed in leaving.

S. Greenbaum and J. Whitcut, Longman Guide to English Usage

---

hopefully

This was the Great Linguistic Bore of the 1980s. People foamed at the mouth over what they declared angrily was the wrong use of hopefully, 'the final descent into darkness for the English language', as one grammarian declared. The first meaning is 'full of hope', as in Robert Louis Stevenson's famous line, 'To travel hopefully is a better thing than to arrive'. The new use meant 'it is hoped': 'Hopefully business will pick up.' There is a technical grammatical objection to this, but 'happily', 'regrettably', 'thankfully' and other words are used in the same way: 'Happily they were able to agree.'

Because it is useful, the alternative use of hopefully gained so much ground that people who hated it at one time often found themselves using it in this way. There are objections, more because of ambiguity than grammar, as in a sentence such as 'We'll set off hopefully tomorrow' (do we hope to set off or shall we be setting off full of hope?). We should be aware of this risk and occasionally substitute 'we hope to' or 'full of hope', to make the meaning clear. But the fuss over this word has died down, and hopefully this will be the last word on the subject.

G. Howard, The Good English Guide

The writers of such guides are calling upon three areas of expertise:

- grammatical knowledge;

- an understanding of the different ways in which language is currently used;

- a sense of style or aesthetics.

In different writers these three are mixed in different proportions.

Other word books

There is a great variety of other alphabetically arranged lists of words providing all sorts of interesting and useful information. Only a small proportion of these are listed here.

Subject dictionaries

Specialist subjects often have an extended and highly technical vocabulary much of which cannot be contained in a standard dictionary. There are often specialist dictionaries devoted to such subjects. For example, the vocabulary of ecology:

---

piezometer   314

over the adjacent lowland or *piedmont zone. Much of the glacier surface is, therefore, at a low altitude and may show rapid *ablation. An example is the Malaspina Glacier, Alaska.

piezometer An observation well designed to measure the elevation of the *water-table or *hydraulic head of *groundwater at a particular level. The well is normally quite narrow and allows groundwater to enter only at a particular depth, rather than throughout its entire length.

piezometric surface See POTENTIO-METRIC SURFACE.

pileus The Latin *pileus*, meaning 'cap' used to describe an accessory cloud occurring as a small cap on or above a cumuliform cloud. The cloud is associated with *cumulus or *cumulonimbus. See also CLOUD CLASSIFICATION.

pillow lava Long piles of basaltic lava pods that have the general appearance of a stack, often many hundreds of metres thick, of discrete stone pillows, each 'pillow' rarely being more than 1 m in diameter. The morphology indicates that the 'pillows' continued to behave as fluid bodies after the chilled carapace had formed. This provides good evidence of submarine eruption: lava entering water acquires a glassy outer skin as heat is conducted rapidly from the surface. Because water absorbs heat more readily than air, with little increase in its own temperature, the rapid surface cooling allows the molten plastic state of the pillow interior to be maintained longer than it would be in air. Pillows have been observed forming under water from lava entering the sea off Hawaii.

pilose Covered with fine hair or down.

pilotage The steering of a course from one place to another by using familiar landmarks.

pine barren An area of pine forest in which the various species of pine usually develop as small or medium-sized trees. The barrens coincide with poor, sandy, and to a lesser extent marshy soil, and owe their ecological character in part to cen-

turies of burning. They occur in the southeastern USA and on the coastal plain of the Atlantic and Gulf of Mexico from New Jersey to Florida (excluding its southern tip) and into Texas.

pin-frame (point frame) A device for obtaining a quantitative estimate of vegetation *cover. Pin-frames are typically made from lightweight wood, aluminium, or plastic and comprise a cross-bar with pin-holes supported on legs of adjustable height. The pin-frame is set up so that the cross-bar sits above the vegetation to be sampled. Pins are lowered through the pin-holes and the plants hit by the pin-tips are recorded. Where the vegetation is of variable height, records of top-cover (the first plant encountered by the pin) and bottom-cover may be taken. The pin diameter used will affect the results and must be standardized for comparative work.

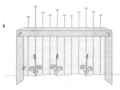

Pin-frame

pingo An ice-cored, dome-shaped hill, oval in plan, 2–50 m high and 30–600 m in diameter, developed in an area of *permafrost. The larger examples have breached crests in which ice may be exposed. They are probably due to local freezing of water that has migrated from adjacent uplands, or to the late freezing of the ground beneath a lake. See also PALSA.

pinnacle reef See REEF.

pinnate Borne on either side of a central stalk; like a feather in appearance.

Pinus aristata See PINUS LONGAEVA.

Pinus longaeva (bristlecone pine) A pine species from California which is

---

33

Spelling dictionaries

If you want to check the spelling of a word you can usually do so in a conventional dictionary. But if you aren't sure how the word begins, this can be time-consuming: for example, how do you spell the word that is pronounced 'sore eye a sis' (psoriasis)? If you know that it begins with a 'p' you probably don't need to check anyway, and looking in a dictionary under 's' won't help at all. A specialist spelling dictionary is organized to help you overcome this problem:

provisions » psych   620

provisions

proviso »*noun* (plural **provisos**) a condition attached to an agreement.
– SAY pruh-vy-zoh

ⓘ **proviso** comes from the Latin phrase *proviso quod*, which means 'it being provided that'
the plural has *os* not *oes*: **provisos**

provocation

provocative
provocatively
provocativeness

provoke (verb: **provokes**, **provoking**, **provoked**)

provost »*noun* ❶ a person in charge of certain university colleges and public schools. ❷ (in Scotland) a mayor.
– SAY pro-vuhst

prow »*noun* the pointed front part of a ship.

prowess »*noun* skill or expertise in a particular activity.

prowl (verb: **prowls**, **prowling**, **prowled**)
prowler

proxies

proximate »*adjective* closest in space, time, or relationship.

proximity »*noun* nearness in space, time, or relationship.

proxy »*noun* (plural **proxies**) ❶ the authority to represent someone else, especially in voting. ❷ a person authorized to act on behalf of another.

Prozac »*noun* (trademark) a drug which is taken to treat depression.

prude »*noun* a person who is easily shocked by matters relating to sex.
prudery
prudish

prudent »*adjective* acting with or showing care and thought for the future.
prudence
prudently

prudential »*adjective* prudent.

prudently
prudery
prudish

prune¹ »*noun* a dried plum.

prune² »*verb* (**prunes**, **pruning**, **pruned**) ❶ trim a tree or bush by cutting away dead or overgrown branches. ❷ remove unwanted parts from.
» *noun* an instance of pruning.

prurient »*adjective* having or encouraging too much interest in sexual matters.

– SAY proor-i-uhnt
prurience
pruriently

pry »*verb* (**pries**, **prying**, **pried**) enquire too eagerly about a person's private life.
prying

PS »*abbreviation* postscript.

psalm »*noun* a song or poem in praise of God, found in the biblical Book of Psalms.
– SAY sahm
psalmist

✓ don't forget the l before the m: **psalm**

psalter »*noun* a book containing the biblical Psalms.
– SAY sawl-ter or sol-ter

psephology »*noun* the statistical study of elections and trends in voting.
– SAY se-fol-uh-ji
psephologist

pseud »*noun* (in informal English) a person who tries to impress others by pretending to have knowledge or expertise they do not really possess.
– SAY syood

pseudo »*adjective* not genuine.
– SAY syoo-doh

pseudo- »*prefix* false; not genuine: *pseudoscience*.

pseudonym »*noun* a false name, especially one used by an author.
– SAY syoo-duh-nim

✓ **nym** not **nim**: **pseudonym**

pseudonymous »*adjective* writing or written under a false name.
– SAY syoo-don-i-muhss
pseudonymously

pseudoscience »*noun* beliefs or practices which may appear scientific but actually are not.
pseudoscientific

psi »*noun* the twenty-third letter of the Greek alphabet (Ψ, ψ).
– SAY psi or si

psoriasis »*noun* a skin disease marked by red, itchy, scaly patches.
– SAY suh-ry-uh-siss

✓ remember, **psoriasis** begins with a silent p, and the ending is **asis**

psych »*verb* (**psychs**, **psyching**, **psyched**) ❶ (**psych up**) prepare someone mentally for a difficult task. ❷ (**psych out**) intimidate an opponent by appearing very confident or aggressive.
– SAY syk

To sum up ...

1 When choosing a dictionary it is important to select one that is big enough to provide all the information you want, but not so big as to be unwieldy and provide information you don't want.

2 Dictionaries are based on the history of how the word has been used in the past, so they can become out of date as language usage changes.

3 A standard dictionary can be expected to provide information about:
- pronunciation
- grammar
- derivation
- meaning
- usage

4 Use a thesaurus to see the range of possible words in a given area of meaning.

5 A thesaurus can be arranged alphabetically but many of the most useful are arranged thematically. To get the best out of these you need to use both the index and the cross-referencing system.

6 Other word reference books include usage dictionaries, subject-specific dictionaries, and spelling dictionaries.

4 | Effective communication

I'm not sure they've quite grasped 'The Waste Land' yet.

Whenever we speak or write we are seeking to communicate with a particular person or group of people. It is essential to think carefully about the needs and situation of that audience when selecting the words we are going to use. To achieve clear communication we need to consider two questions:

■ How well can they understand the language?

■ How much do they know about the subject?

How well can they understand the language?

A good way to understand clearly what is involved is to compare three texts on the same subject written for different audiences:

1

> Claude spent his last years at home in Giverny...Many of Claude's last works were huge paintings of waterlilies. In this painting [illustration] it is hard to tell where the lilies end and their reflections begin.

1

Sean Connolly, *The Life and Work of Claude Monet*, Heinnemann Library 1999

This extract is from an information book for young children. The sentences are short and the words are simple (the most difficult are 'waterlilies' and 'reflections'.

2

> The water lily paintings are often considered by art historians to be the greatest paintings of Monet's career. In 1883 he rented a house at Giverny, fifty miles from Paris. Seven years later he purchased the house and shortly afterwards in 1893 purchased a meadow near the property which contained a pond fed by the Ru River, a tributary of the Seine. He employed at least six gardeners who gradually shaped the meadow into a garden of willows, irises and water lilies specially imported from Japan. Monet painted the gardens around the house.

2

Monet
ticktock Publishing 1997

Here the sentences are considerably longer, and the vocabulary is more demanding, with words like 'considered', purchased', and 'tributary'.

3

> The idea of combining a group of water landscapes to form a complete and encompassing environment probably entered Monet's mind during (if not before) the exhibition of 1909 ; lonely and discouraged after the death of his second wife in 1911, he all but ceased to paint. By the time the Venetian series was finished, a cataract had already begun to form over one eye. Before the war came the death of his son Jean, whose wife, Blanche Hoschedé, became his assistant, painting companion, and protector. It was not she, however, but Clemenceau who finally roused him from mourning and inactivity…

3

William C. Seitz, *Monet*
Thames & Hudson 1984

In this extract the sentences are longer again. They are also more complex. The vocabulary, too, has moved on. Now the reader is asked to read and understand: 'encompassing', 'environment', discouraged', and 'cataract'. These words are not only longer, but more technical ('cataract') or intellectually more specialized ('encompassing').

So readability is affected by a combination of features:

■ sentence length;

■ sentence complexity;

■ vocabulary.

Although the grammar and structure of speech differ from those of writing, many points apply to both. The comments that follow refer specifically to reading, but most of them apply equally to listening.

What makes words 'easy' or 'difficult'?

zeugma /ˈzjuːgmə/
• n. a figure of speech in which a word applies to two others in different senses (e.g. *John and his driving licence expired last week*).

Concise Oxford on CD-ROM

It would be convenient if you could say that the shorter a word is the easier it is for an inexperienced reader. Unfortunately, a glance at the dictionary will show that this is not the case. Many children will recognize 'television' and 'elephant' quite early in their reading careers, while they will struggle with 'crypt' or 'zeugma'. On the other hand, many short words are common and easily recognized: 'cat', 'dog', and 'table' are obviously easier than 'lioness', 'hyena', and 'escritoire'.

The features that seem to be important in selecting words according to the reading skills of your audience are:

■ length and structure;

■ how common they are in the texts that these readers are familiar with.

Length and structure

If you look at the kind of books that children learn to read from (or those used with adult literacy classes) you will find that many of the words are not just short but also have a simple pattern. Many of the first words encountered have:

■ one syllable (e.g. 'boy', 'cow');

■ only one or two consonant letters at the beginning (or none at all) (e.g. 'big', 'clap', 'eat');

■ only one or two consonant letters at the end (e.g. 'man', 'want').

The reason for this is that children learn to read words in two ways: by recognizing the whole word from its context and shape and by sounding it out, turning the individual letters or groups of letters into sounds—'c-a-t cat'. The sounding out method means that many of the early words are as mentioned above.

Familiarity

Children and adults learning to read English learn both from the special reading materials they use at school and from the world of print they see all around them. Reading schemes for children naturally reflect the real world they live in and their imaginative world. At the same time children also read 'real' texts, and will pick up and try to read anything that they find around them. So alongside words like 'adventure' and 'dragon' they will meet 'millionaire', 'quiz', and even 'premiership'.

Adults who are slow readers will, of course, have a vocabulary that is similarly limited but which covers different areas of experience. Young children might be able to read the word 'tax', but probably won't know what it means. Adults know only too well!

The **British National Corpus** is a set of English texts that reflect the range of ways English is used. It is possible to work out how frequently common words are used and put them in rank order:

1	the
2	be
3	of
101	find
102	man
1001	useful
1002	extent
5001	regulatory
5002	cylinder

As a general rule, when writing for either group you should aim to select words that are in common everyday use, since there is a much higher chance that your readers will have met them before and will be able to read and understand them. The more experienced your audience are as readers, the more complex words you can afford to use.

This can pose difficult problems. The commonest words are often the most general. Compare these three sentences:

> They bought a dog.
> They bought a pointer.
> They bought a Weimaraner.

If it doesn't matter what kind of dog has been bought, then the first sentence is fine, but for a dog specialist only the last, and most difficult, word will do. So you may find you have to make compromises between the **precise** word and the **readable** word.

Making 'readable' not mean 'vague'

Fortunately language is flexible, and there are usually ways round a problem. We can nearly always add information. An obvious way of doing this is to use illustrations. Some manufacturers have developed this to a high level, and supply instructions for their products containing no words at all.

Another solution is to provide your own explanation or gloss of the difficult word:

Don't insult your audience

It might appear that the best way to play safe is always to use simple language and short sentences. This would certainly ensure that everyone could read what you wrote, but it would also run a serious risk of alienating your audience, some of whom might feel that you were talking down to them. Writing can never be a 'one size fits all' business. Despite what some advocates of 'plain English' might assert, you always have to give careful thought to the precise needs and skills of your audience. The sentence above, explaining what a Weimaraner is, would be fine for a children's book, but it would certainly not be suitable in an article written for dog breeders!

How much do they know?

As the last example shows, the choice of words is not just about how well your audience can read; it also concerns how much they know about the subject. Different readers bring different levels of knowledge to reading a text. With knowledge comes the vocabulary to express it. You can check this for yourself by thinking about a subject you are interested in. Think back to when you first became aware of it and then run through the process by which you gradually learned more about it. You will very probably find that as your knowledge about it increased, so did the store of words to describe it.

Suppose, for example, you are a keen photographer. You might have started out with a small, simple camera, the type they sometimes call 'point-and-shoot'. You will only have needed a fairly simple vocabulary. For example:

brightness	develop	film
flash	print	shutter release

As you became more skilled and experienced, however, you probably bought a larger and more complicated camera and learned to compose your pictures and control your exposures with more skill. For this you would need terms like:

aperture	depth of field	exposure
filter	focal length	

Increasing knowledge and understanding leads to the use of even less common terms:

acutance	colour cast	gamma

If you wish to write about a technical subject like photography you have to decide where your readers are on this learning curve and, therefore, how many of the technical terms they may be expected to know. Those that are unlikely to be familiar need to be explained when they are first introduced, and possibly included in a glossary to which users can refer while reading the text. (Remember that it is unlikely that readers will grasp fully the meaning of a term after only one explanation.)

It is, of course, difficult to think of all this while you are writing. It is better to write the text bearing in mind the kind of person you are addressing (and the answers to the two questions listed on page 36), but not stopping to question every word. When you read through what you have written, you can then check specifically for the level of the language you have used, making explanations and changes as necessary.

To sum up ...

1 When writing or speaking, think of your audience.

2 Choose words that are suited to your readers' or listeners' language skills.

3 Think also about how much knowledge they have of the subject, and choose words, especially technical terms, carefully.

4 If you need to use words that may be unfamiliar, try to build in an explanation of their meaning.

5 On the other hand, do not patronize your audience by using words that they will find babyish.

5 When the words get in the way

In the previous chapter we looked at how to communicate efficiently, by using words that are pitched at the right linguistic and technical level for the audience. But as well as being aware of people's intellectual needs, we also need to take into account their personal and emotional needs as individuals.

When you speak to someone, or present them with words to read, you are, to a degree, intruding upon their lives. This is particularly true if your audience is unknown to you personally. If you choose the right words you can get them on your side, but if you choose the wrong words you can alienate them so that whatever you say will fall on deaf ears.

Formal or informal?

Look at these three greetings:

■ Good morning.

■ Hullo.

■ Hi!

Each is suitable for certain occasions but not all. If you know the person you are addressing very little, if at all, then 'Good morning' is a suitable greeting. If, on the other hand, you know the person very well, you are less likely to use it, or, if you do, you may well shorten it to 'Morning'. 'Hi!', on the other hand is considerably less formal and, therefore, less suitable for greeting someone you have never met before. This kind of usage, however, is not fixed and depends on both individual taste and changing fashion. For example, people who have never met or corresponded before are not unlikely to use 'Hi!' as a greeting in emails. The example illustrates two key points about formality:

- It is linked to how well you know the audience.

- It is a matter of personal experience and choice.

You might assume that with an unknown audience you would always be formal in your choice of language and that you should never be formal with those you know well.

How formal do you want to be?

In fact it is quite easy to think of occasionas when this 'rule' should be broken. If you write stories for young children, for example, you are probably writing for an audience you do not know personally, but you will get through to them much more directly and immediately if you adopt an informal style. To go to the opposite extreme, the principal of a college might adopt a formal tone when addressing the whole student body, even though she may know many of them quite well—and would address them more informally when speaking one-to-one. We can represent this in a diagram:

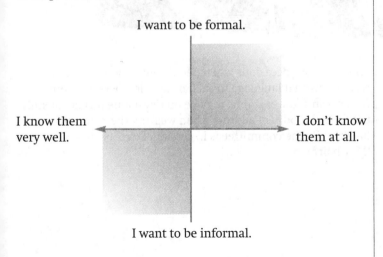

I want to be formal.

I know them very well.   I don't know them at all.

I want to be informal.

Anything you say or write for an audience can be plotted somewhere on the diagram on page 45, and although the majority of situations will be placed in the shaded areas, a number will fall well outside them. Two examples of this have already been given. Another common situation when people unknown to each other use informal language is correspondence by email. Indeed, the Internet as a whole invites informal language usage. Another medium which makes considerable use of infomal language for addressing total strangers is advertising.

There are also occasions when people who know each other well use formal language to each other. Members of a committee or board, for example, may be on first-name terms but still use formal modes of address when wearing their 'committee hats': while the committee is in session 'Dave' becomes 'Mr Chairman'.

What do we mean by formal and informal vocabulary?

As we saw earlier, this is partly a matter of personal experience and choice. Most of the time we choose words intuitively, without spending a lot of time agonizing over the choice. But not always. So it is good practice to be aware of the ways in which people use words—and the situations in which they use them. The more you observe and reflect upon how other people use words, the more confident you will become about your own speaking and writing.

It is useful to get into the habit of placing groups of words with related meanings on a scale that runs from formal to informal. The following list of words has been taken from a thesaurus:

mean   parsimonious   stingy   tight-arsed   ungenerous

We could arrange them like this:

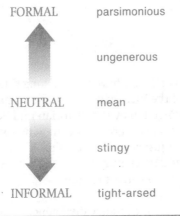

FORMAL	parsimonious
	ungenerous
NEUTRAL	mean
	stingy
INFORMAL	tight-arsed

You try

How would you grade this group of words?

dead duck	failure
defeatist	loser
drag	melancholic
drongo	no-hoper
Eeyore	pessimist

47

Words and social groups

You sometimes hear people say, 'It's not a word I would use in polite society.' This is a rather coy thing to say—sometimes it is said with a joky, fake coyness—but it recognizes an important feature of the way we use words. Our vocabulary is often determined by the social groups we belong to. We can see this particularly in four key areas of language: taboo, euphemism, slang, and jargon.

Taboo

Linguists use this term to refer to expressions that are considered unacceptable in 'polite society'. This is frequently because of their subject matter. Taboo subjects in the past have included:

- sexual activity;

- excretion;

- death.

The English in particular have taken a long time to shake off the hypocrisy of the Victorian age. (While all manner of sexual activity was indulged in by the Victorian middle classes, sex was something that was not, in the drawing room, admitted to exist.) But it isn't just sex that causes problems. Even at the beginning of the 21st century there are those who find it difficult to talk about cancer, for example.

In these areas there is a strange divergence of language. It seems that you can either talk about them coarsely or obliquely. Direct reference is much more difficult. Take excretion, for example. The direct words, 'shit' and 'piss' have been downgraded to 'coarse', so most people fall back on circumlocution: 'wash my hands', 'powder my nose', 'go to the loo', etc.
The same applies to the extraordinary lengths we go to when referring to the place used. Even 'lavatory' (which refers to washing rather than excretion) is considered too much by many people who prefer 'toilet', 'loo', and 'bathroom'.

Euphemisms

When we avoid direct reference to taboo subjects, we use words and expressions called 'euphemisms'. For example, people don't die, they 'pass on', 'pass away', or simply 'go'. Similarly with illness. Cancer is 'the big C'; if the doctor wishes to enquire whether a patient has problems with passing water or 'urination' the question may well be put as 'Any trouble with the waterworks?'

Another way of concealing the unpalatable truth is to use jargon. When companies wish to dismiss an employee they often use language that attempts to tone down or even disguise the effects of their actions. They may speak of 'dispensing with his services', or 'offering a career change opportunity'. Other terms to describe sacking someone include:

destaffing	downsizing	outplacement
negotiated	departure	workforce adjustment

Governments have, over the years, been particularly adept at using words to conceal what they are up to. The nuclear power industry is fairly good at it too. In the late 1970s, when there was an explosion at the nuclear power station on Three Mile Island in the USA, it was referred to as, among other things, 'an energetic disassembly', and the fire that ensued as 'a rapid oxidation'.

Slang

Slang is often used by members of a particular group, so there are different types of slang, for example schoolboy slang. The members of the group enjoy using their own special vocabulary which bonds them as a group and may be mildly mystifying to outsiders. Slang is also subject to fashion; words come and go, and what was yesterday's 'in' word marks you down as out of touch if you use it today. You only have to look at the range of words used by young people to express approval to see the truth of this. In the past these have included 'cool', 'brill', 'heavy', 'ace', 'triff', 'def', 'wicked', and 'awesome'. (There is no point in attempting to comment on what is current, because by the time this book is published it won't be.)

Not all slang is confined to particular groups. Most people use slang at times. And not all slang is equally acceptable in all social situations. While it is perfectly acceptable to refer to a *couch potato* in polite society, the use of a term such as *pissed* (for 'drunk') is less generally acceptable. At that point slang has moved into the area of 'taboo'.

It's the police!

As an example of the rich variety of slang, here are just some of the words that have been applied to police officers or special groups of them over the years in the United Kingdom and the United States:

bobby	bogey	busy	copper
dick	filth	fuzz	grog
hawkshaw	mingra	mug	peeler
pigs	plod	plod	rozzer
scuffer	shamus	sweeney	the law
the man			

Jargon

In Chapter 4 we looked at the use of technical terms. It isn't easy to pinpoint where 'technical terms' become 'jargon'. As we have seen, technical terminology is necessary, although one has to bear in mind the needs of the audience. The best way to see how jargon works is to look at a few examples:

> Compositing is the process of blending different video clips. It's very similar to working with layers, except that After Effects gives you finer control over how the different components can be blended. After Effects enables you to create different compositions using filters, mattes, and other techniques and then combine these into a single result.

Here the writer is forced to use a number of technical terms because of the subject matter. Words like 'filter' and 'matte' are part of the terminology of the subject. So while some may find the text verging on jargon, it is difficult to see what else the writer could have done.

> A perfect pole water, nine metres puts you tight to the central island. In summer, use pellet and paste on a short line. Pleasure bags regularly exceed 100lb. Best warm water pegs are the shallows, pegs 10-13. It's mostly silver fish in winter to maggot or pinkie. Liquidised bread and punch takes nets to double figures.

Here there are technical terms which may be necessary (e.g. 'barbless'). Some words are being used in a specialized way (e.g. 'pegs'), while others are clearly a kind of enthusiasts' slang ('pinkies', 'punch'). The heavy concentration of this specialist vocabulary is to provide a kind of bonding for readers in the know and to exclude outsiders.

> The first nose is distinctly of baked parsnips: quite waxy with a hint of Vick's vapour rub. Water introduces a melange of carpenter's shop aromas (sawdust, shavings, simple glue) and perhaps a fresh pea pod note.

In this final extract, there are almost no technical terms and most of the words used are very ordinary. What makes it a piece of jargon is the way in which ordinary words have been used. The overall effect is no doubt fascinating to insiders (lovers of scotch malt whisky) but rather bizarre to those who are outside the chosen group.

If your intention as a writer or speaker is to maintain a clique and turn your back on 'outsiders', well and good. If not, then you need to ask yourself, 'Which of these special words I am using are necessary technical terms, and which are unnecessary jargon?'

Business speak

Jargon is everywhere and people are fascinated by it. (Try keying in 'jargon' on any web search engine, and you will see what I mean.) Nowhere is it more prevalent than in business, where some executives can use it to say nothing in a thousand words. What follows is part of a statement from a company called Unicorp. It's a parody...or is it?

Unicorp: Dedicated to Excellence

One of Unicorp's corporate objectives is to develop strategic relationships with key customers and be recognized for our ability to deliver services of superior value. This competitive advantage will be achieved through continued focus on our core competencies, management attention to the development of operations and process management excellence in all parts of our business, the identification and application of best processes, and continued attention to direct and indirect cost management. The focus on core competencies will promote the concentration of knowledge in select areas consistent with the tenets of Unicorp's strategic plan, Unicorp 2000. Management's attention to operations and process management excellence in all business areas will be achieved through the continued expansion of our management and technical staff, as well as through consistent application of corporate quality programs such as benchmarking and continuous improvement, leading to the establishment of Unicorp's superior business processes in each core competency. Finally, continued attention to direct and indirect cost management will enable Unicorp to offer customers a superior, value-added package of high-quality service at a competitive price.

Corporate Mission

Our multi-faceted mission is our driving force. Unicorp wants to:

1. Establish solid corporate leadership which guides and directs the effective accomplishment of strategic goals and objectives;

2. Foster an attitude of outstanding customer service and satisfaction;

3. Continually refine our corporate vision to leverage our human, technical, and financial resources effectively to achieve strategic goals;

4. Instill a corporate atmosphere, management philosophy, and organizational performance criteria which capitalizes on diversity;

5. Promote a commitment to outstanding performance, quality, innovation, and pursuit of excellence; and

6. Maintain a people-come-first environment where all employees are integral components of our success formula.

With thanks to Steven Morgan Friedman. The whole text can be found at http://www.westegg.com/jargon/

Connotations

Earlier we saw that words can differ not only in their differing degrees of formality; some words, like 'mean', can also tell us about the speaker's attitude towards the subject. It is often the case that we can choose between words that are favourable to the subject, neutral words, and those that are critical or even hostile. For example:

The room was bijou, cool, and not over-lit.
The room was small, cold, and dark
The room was poky, chilly, and dingy

All three provide the same basic information about the room, but while the first sets out to present a favourable picture of it, the third makes it seem as unpleasant as possible. The middle one is broadly neutral.

So words not only have a dictionary meaning, they also have connotations, and we need to be aware of this when we choose.

... and here is your residence: bijou, cool and not overlit

Bias

The connotations of some words can communicate personal, social, or political prejudice. This is sometimes deliberate and sometimes not. Some bias is built into the language, as in the case of words containing 'man'. In Old English the word 'man' meant person, and there were separate words for male person and female person. Of these only 'woman' has survived, while 'man' has come to mean specifically 'male person'. If you wish to be even-handed and not discriminate against half the population, you have problems with expressions such as:

be one's own man	businessman
chairman	Englishman
every man for himself	foreman
man hours	mankind
man-made	manpower
man-to-man	policeman
fireman	the common man

There is no single solution to this. A common approach is to replace 'man' with 'person'. This works well for a number of the expressions above: 'man-to-man' can be replaced by 'person-to-person', for example. In other cases it can appear slightly awkward ('chairperson'), strange ('policeperson'), or absurd ('be one's own person'). The following are possible alternatives:

Original	Alternative
be one's own man	be true to oneself
chairman	chair
every man for himself	everybody for themselves
man hours	staff/working time
man-made	synthetic/manufactured
man-to-man	person-to-person/one-to-one
fireman	fire fighter
businessman	business executive
Englishman/men	English person/the English
foreman	supervisor/charge hand
manpower	staff
policeman	police officer
the common man	the ordinary person

He or she?

The other problem that English poses for those who wish to avoid a sexist bias in speech or writing is that it lacks a neuter personal pronoun. How do you fill the gaps in the following sentence so that it applies equally to men and women?

Anyone who wishes to apply for this post must send a copy of _____ CV with details of _____ current salary.

We have only the choice of 'his' or 'her'. One way is to use 'his or her' for each space, but this is rather clumsy. A better way is to rewrite the sentence. There are four ways of doing this:

1 **Turn it into the plural**
   Those who wish to apply for this post must send copies of their CVs with details of their current salaries.

2 **Make it into direct address**
   If you wish to apply for this post you must send a copy of your CV with details of your current salary.

3 **Make it passive**
   Applications for this post must be accompanied by a copy of the applicant's current CV and details of current salary.

4 **Use 'their' instead of 'his' or 'her'**
   Anyone who wishes to apply for this post must send copies of their CV with details of their current salary.

They all have advantages and disadvantages. The first is slightly awkward because it could be understood that each applicant has more than one CV. The second is accurate but less formal than some writers would like—but it is an increasingly common approach. The third is very formal and so would not appeal to many writers. The fourth is an increasingly popular solution, although traditionalists disapprove because they argue that 'their' must always refer back to more than one person (which 'anyone' clearly is not). Ultimately this is a matter of personal judgement and taste.

Other bias

Linguistic prejudice against women is not, of course, the only one. Other groups who can be and often are discriminated against through choice of words include:

- people from different ethnic or religious groups;
- homosexuals;
- those who are physically or mentally handicapped;
- the old.

To sum up ...

1 The words we use have an impact on people well beyond their literal meanings.

2 One way of categorizing words is by considering how formal or informal they are.

3 In general we use more formal words with people whom we do not know and/or whom we do not wish to offend.

4 Informal language is most safely used with people you know well.

5 Some words are considered unacceptable in 'polite society'. They are known as 'taboo' words. The membership of this group of words changes with time.

6 When people are embarassed by a subject or the words needed to talk about it, they may use a more 'polite' or less 'offensive' word. This is called euphemism.

7 The special informal vocabulary of particular groups is known as slang.

8 Special use of technical words by an 'in-group' of experts or enthusiasts in a particular subject is called jargon. It may alienate outsiders, sometimes deliberately.

9 Jargon is also sometimes used deliberately to conceal the truth.

10 Words can also indicate, explicitly or implicitly, bias against particular social groups such as women, ethnic minorities, or the old.

6

Where do English words come from?

Over the centuries the English language has been influenced by the history of the peoples who speak it and by the languages of the many different countries with which they have come into contact. That last sentence contains words that come from Old English (over), Latin (century), and French (language). In this chapter we look at some of the main influences on English and examine where English words come from.

Early influences

The earliest inhabitants of the British Isles were Celtic and it is surprising that very few words survive from this period into modern English. Of these the most widely known today are probably 'crag' and 'brock' (as a name for badger). The Isles were conquered by the Romans, and a number of Latin words in modern English are to be found in Old English. They include a number of everyday words:

belt	candle	cat	cheese
dish	kettle	pea	plant
shirt	street	wall	wine

Many other Latin words, however, came into English at a later date, as we shall see.

Old English

The story of the English language really begins in the 5th century AD, when invaders from what is now northern Germany and Denmark began to attack the east and south coasts of Britain.

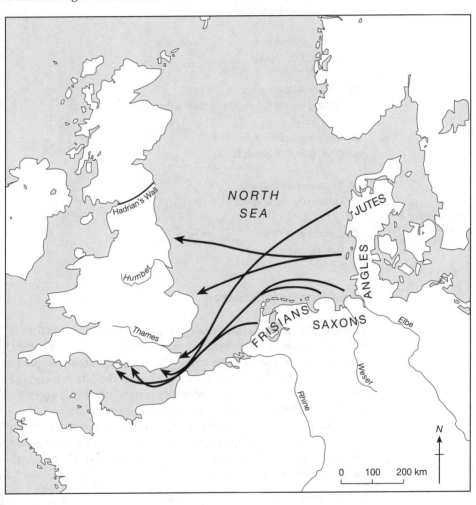

These Angles, Saxons, and Jutes soon began to settle, and gradually conquered much of what we now call England. Their language was Germanic in origin, and many of the commonest words in Modern English date right back to Old English (or Anglo-Saxon, as it is sometimes called).

Old English words

These include words for:

- Parts of the body
  hand, foot, arm, ankle

- Household things
  house, floor, door

- Family relationships
  father, mother, son, daughter, wife

- Common animals
  cow, horse, hound, fox

- Common adjectives
  small, old, new, great

- Common verbs
  run, go, walk

See Chapter 8
and Glossary for
an explanation of
grammatical terms
used in this chapter.

Scandinavian influences

During the Anglo-Saxon period, England was subject to other
invasions from north-west Europe. Waves of invaders variously
described as Danes, Norsemen, and Vikings (or 'creek people')
attached the east and south coasts between the late 8th and the
early 11th centuries. Their influence is most obviously seen
in the differences between the place names of northern and
eastern England, where they settled, and southern and western
place names where they did not penetrate. A very typical group
of Scandinavian-style place names end in 'by' and other typical
endings are '-thorpe', '-thwaite', and '-toft'.

Examples

Rugby	Naseby	Lowestoft
Grimethorpe	Bassenthwaite	

Common English words with a Scandinavian origin include:

again	anger	bag	bank
cake	die	dirt	egg
flat	fog	get	happy
husband	law	leg	neck
off	seat	seem	smile
steak	take	want	window

6 Where do English words come from?

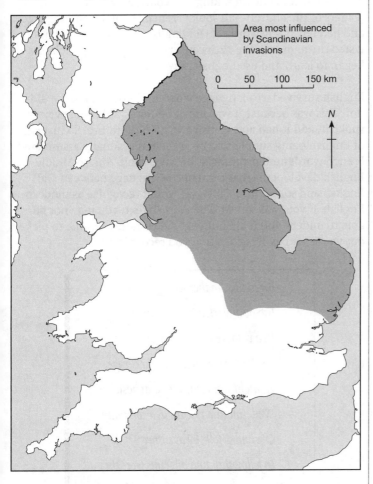

Area most influenced by Scandinavian invasions

0   50   100   150 km

N

Although the Scandinavians did leave a mark on the English language, their influence was relatively small—especially when compared with the effects of the next major invasion, that of the Normans.

Middle English

The development of the English language was changed radically by the Norman Conquest of the 11th century. A group of warriors from northern France attacked and defeated the Saxon army, led by King Harold, near Hastings in 1066. Their native tongue was French and this became the language of the ruling class for centuries: king and court, great landowners, the leaders of the church—all spoke French as their first language and had few if any words of Old English. This state of affairs lasted through into the 12th century, when the upper classes began to learn and use English as well as French.

English survived as a language whereas Celtic (and Latin) did not. This was because it was much better established: everyone spoke it, and it had an extensive written literature. So instead of English being supplanted by French, it gradually assimilated French words (and pronunciation) into itself. And so Middle English developed—that form of the language between Old English and something which we would recognize as modern English. If you look at a Middle English text, you may not be able to understand it all, but you will certainly be able to pick out words and expressions that you recognize:

> *Befell that, in that season on a day,*
> *In Southwark at the Tabard as I lay,*
> *Ready to wenden on my pilgrimage*
> *To Canterbury with devout corage,*
> *At night was come into that hostelry*
> *Well nine and twenty in a company*
> *Of sundry folk, by aventure y-fall*
> *In fellowship, and pilgrims were they all,*
> *That toward Canterbury woulde ride.*

from the General Prologue to the *Canterbury Tales* by Geoffrey Chaucer (1340–1400)

The influence of French

It was only to be expected that the biggest single influence on Middle English was Norman French. French-derived words commonly in use today cover many different aspects of life:

Government and law

accuse	arrest	authority	blame
convict	council	crime	fine
fraud	government	judge	jury
libel	liberty	minister	pardon
prison	punishment	tax	verdict

Food and drink

bacon	beef	biscuit	cream
dinner	fruit	gravy	lemon
lettuce	mustard	mutton	orange
pigeon	pork	roast	salad
saucer	stew	sugar	supper
toast	vinegar		

Household things

basin	blanket	chair	chimney
couch	curtain	cushion	lamp
latch	pantry	porch	towel

Other everyday words

action	age	air	allow
blue	change	country	cry
easy	enter	face	final
honest	hour	move	noise
order	pass	people	perfect
poor	receive	reply	safe
save	simple	solid	

Latin

If French was the first language of the Anglo-Norman Establishment, its second was Latin. Latin was the language of the Church, all of whose services and administration were conducted in it. It was also the language of the laws, so it is not surprising that many words referring to government and law are Latin in origin:

alias	client	conviction	homicide
legal	prosecute	testify	

Other Latin introductions from this period are:

admit	collision	comet	contempt
contradiction	depression	desk	discuss
exclude	expedition	explicit	formal
genius	history	imaginary	include
index	interest	interrupt	moderate
necessary	nervous	picture	popular

Duplication

This wealth of words from different sources meant that English often has two or more words that mean much the same thing. For example:

begin/commence
help/aid
hide/conceal
wedding/marriage
wish/desire

It also gave rise to the often-noted fact that while our words for common farm animals come from Old English, those for the meat they provide come from Norman French:

ox/beef
sheep/mutton
pig/pork

Early Modern English

The period of the Renaissance, from the late 15th to the mid-17th centuries, saw an enormous expansion of learning and the arts. At the same time speakers of English travelled not only across Europe but also to the Far East and to the New World. One result of this was a massive expansion of the vocabulary.

Words from Latin and Greek

absurd	adapt	appropriate	assassinate
atmosphere	autograph	benefit	climax
conspicuous	crisis	emphasis	encyclopaedia
enthusiasm	exact	explain	external
fact	harass	malignant	monopoly
parasite	pathetic	relaxation	scheme
temperature	tonic		

Words from French

anatomy	bizarre	chocolate	detail
duel	entrance	equip	explore
invite	muscle	passport	progress
shock	ticket	tomato	vase

Words from Italian

balcony	carnival	design	fuse
giraffe	lottery	opera	rocket
sonnet	volcano		

Plus, of course, many of the words used in music: 'concerto', 'piano', 'solo', 'sonata', 'soprano', and 'violin', for example.

Words from Spanish and Portuguese

anchovy   apricot   banana   barricade

cannibal   canoe   cocoa   embargo

guitar   hammock   hurricane   mosquito

potato   tank   tobacco

Words from elsewhere in Europe

cruise   easel   horde   landscape

ombudsman   sauna   ski   trousers

Words from India

pyjama   jungle   bungalow   thug

Words from elsewhere in Asia

bamboo   ketchup   tycoon

Words from the Near and Middle East

caravan   coffee   jackal   kiosk

Words from elsewhere around the world

cannibal   potato   safari   taboo

voodoo   zero

Modern English

The process of adding new words has continued undiminished to the present day. New words come into English in a number of ways

Loan words

As in the past, many new words are simply borrowed from other languages. These are referred to as loan words.

English is a world language, so it is unsurprising that it borrows words from all over the world. Sometimes it is fairly obvious where a word comes from, sometimes less so. You might like to work out where each of these words originated:

anorak	assassin	cellar	chutney
corgi	cravat	gimmick	gong
intelligentsia	jackal	mumps	poppycock
robot	shampoo	trek	

Invented words

In some walks of life it has been necessary to manufacture words to fulfil specific purposes. The sciences have been particularly prolific. Many scientific words are built up from Greek and Latin roots. Many are well known. 'ology' at the end of a word denotes 'the study of', while anything with 'bio' in it has to do with life and 'gynae' in a word signifies that it has to do with women.

There is more about new words in the next chapter, Newspeak

Other scientific words derive wholly or in part from the names of scientists involved in a particular study. So, for example, *volts* are named after the Italian scientist Alessandro Volta, and *joules* after the English physicist J. P. Joule.

Compounds

Compounding is the process by which two words are combined to form a new word. For example:

paperknife   darkroom

Each of these compounds is made from two other words but has a meaning that is different from the combined meaning of the two. A paperknife, for example is not a knife made of paper, but one used for cutting paper. Similarly there is a big difference—as any photographer will tell you—between a dark room and a darkroom. (The fact that these are two different concepts is highlighted by the fact that we pronounce them differently, too.)

Compounds can sometimes make you think twice when writing. Is it 'paper knife', 'paper-knife', or 'paperknife'? In fact all three can be found in dictionaries. The history of a typical compound is that it starts off being written as two separate words, then is hyphenated, and ends as a single word.

Most compounds are nouns or adjectives. They are formed in a large number of ways, and the examples that follow cover only a few of these.

Many compound nouns are based on a combination of a noun and a verb. If your head aches, for example, you have a headache, and if the frost bites you, frostbite may follow. If you control yourself, you have self-control (and there are a number of similar compounds starting 'self-'), the art of keeping financial records or 'books' is book-keeping, while something that scares crows is a scarecrow. Sometimes these compounds describe a characteristic behaviour: a man who watches is a watchman, and a boy who plays is a playboy. As these examples show, the two elements can be in either order. Other compounds link two nouns where one of them does something to the other one. Thus a windmill is something where the wind works the mill, a silkworm is a worm that makes silk, and a postman is a man who delivers the post.

Some compound adjectives combine a noun and a verb: heart-breaking and breathtaking. Others are formed of an adverb plus a verb: everlasting and well-meaning. Other compound adjectives combine a noun and an adjective, for example home-sick (=sick for home, rather than sick of home!) and watertight. They are commonly formed to describe colours, rose-red and other physical qualities, ice-cold.

To sum up ...

1 The basis of modern English is old English or Anglo-Saxon. This was a Germanic language spoken by the invaders of the 5th century AD.

2 The language was influenced slightly by the Scandinavian invasions during the 8th, 9th, 10th, and 11th centuries.

3 The next major influence was Norman French, the language of the 11th-century conquerors of England.

4 Latin also had a significant impact on English both indi-rectly, via Norman French, and directly, because it was the language of the Church during the medieval period.

5 This variety of influences has meant that English often has two or more words with the same meaning or similar meanings.

6 Between 1450 and 1650 English borrowed many more words from classical Greek and Latin, French, Italian, Spanish, and Portuguese.

7 More recently, words have come into the language from all over the world.

8 The development of science and other academic disciplines has led to a considerable expansion of the vocabulary as new words are constructed to express new concepts.

9 Words also continue to be constructed by the process of compounding, in which two existing words are combined to make a new one.

7 | Newspeak

In his prophetic novel *Nineteen Eighty-Four* George Orwell warned that central governments might become so powerful that by controlling language itself they would be able to control the way we think. He noted that we had a 'Ministry of Defence' which might more accurately be described as a 'Ministry of War', and projected this idea into a 'Big Brother' state where vocabulary was constantly modified. As changes were introduced, bureaucrats sifted through all print documents, removing old, unacceptable words and replacing them with new.

While Orwell was right in suspecting the motives of governments and other large organization where language is concerned, he failed to foresee the impact popular culture and globalization would have on words. Speakers of English today are subjected to a torrent of new words and phrases, many of which are at first sight incomprehensible and few of which will survive long enough to make it into a dictionary. For example, the excellent website logophilia.com lists hundred of new words observed in print and electronic media, and is adding to them all the time. Among its 'Top 50' at the time of writing were:

evangineer	alpha pup	plunderphonics
McMansion	crapshoot economics	asymmetric
warfare	coffeehousing	text literacy
advergame	one-banana problem	yottabyte
bubble tea	bar-code hairstyle	Web bug
debt porn	geocaching	war driving
eco-porn	firing squad photo	Napster bomb
google	PowerPointlessness	snert
tankini	gaydar	Generation D
obesogenic	ICU psychosis	active aging
extreme gardening	scarlet-collar worker	packet monkey

The first thing to observe about these words is that few of them are really unfamiliar. That is to say, that they are constructed by combining whole words that are relatively common, or parts of common words. Even those that look unfamiliar are often made from bits that we would recognize in other words. You may not know *obesogenic*, but you probably know **obes**ity and carcino**genic**. So it is the combination of familar parts that creates the unfamiliarity.

Sometimes, as with *obesogenic,* we can guess at a word's meaning. But with other new compounds we may lack the necessary context or reference to make sense of them. For example, unless you are familar with the world of software engineers and their feelings of contempt for those who do not inhabit their world ('monkeys'), you will not realize that the expression 'one-banana problem' is used to mean a simple task—one that will only take a 'monkey' one banana to solve. (By analogy, presumably with Sherlock Holmes's 'one-pipe problems'.)

A one-banana problem

| **Filling the gaps**

Sometimes a concept has existed for some time, but there has been no single word with which to express it. People made do with constructing a suitable phrase until someone came up with the bright idea of a single word that would do the job. For example, bats map the world around them by sending out high-pitched signals which are reflected back. The length of time the sound takes to return tells them how far away the object is. But there was no single word to express how bats 'see' things until the 1940s, when the word *echolocate* was coined.

More frequently a new concept arrives on the scene and it becomes necessary to create a word or phrase with which to express it. The Internet has spawned dozens of such words. In a recent newsletter the editors of the *Oxford English Dictionary* listed (among others) the following as new words:

cookie	cybercafe	cybercrime	cyberphobia
cyberporn	dot com	emoticon	FAQ
hyperlink	hypertext	internetworking	spamming
webcam	web-enabled	webzine	

Many of these are now common currency, and by the time this book is published many more Internet-related new words will no doubt have appeared on the scene.

Another area of rapid technological growth is where science and farming meet. We no longer bother to refer to 'genetically modified' crops, simply calling them as 'GM crops'. But other words are appearing which are less common. Among them is 'pharmer'. This term was explained by Michael Behe in 'Darwin's Black Box': 'Designed plants that resist frost or insect pests have been around for a while now; somewhat newer is the engineering of cows that give milk containing large amounts of useful proteins. (The people who do this by inject-ing extraneous genes into cow embryos like to call themselves 'pharmers', short for pharmaceutical farmers.)'

New words as comments

In the examples above, the new words were created because there was a clear need. The lack of them was inhibiting useful dialogue. Often, however, people invent words and phrases partly to aid clear communication but also partly to make a comment on a new phenomenon. This was the impetus that led to words like 'yuppy' and 'nimby' a few years ago. More recently we have seen:

- adhocracy
  an organization which, far from being highly structured and bureaucratic, has just developed in a haphazard and ad hoc way;

- dadrock
  Rock music performed by (or for?) members of the older generation—e.g. ageing rock stars;

- eco-porn
  the use of advertising by large commercial corporations to tell the world how environmentally concerned they are;

- nannycam
  affluent people who employ a nanny to look after their children sometimes don't trust them. So they conceal a tiny video camera in a toy or some other place where it can spy on their nanny;

- plutography
  the genre of writing that focuses on the lives and lifestyles of the very wealthy;

- permalancer
  a freelance worker who has worked so long for one company as to become in effect a permanent employee;

- slackademic
  a perpetual student—the academic life as a way of avoiding real work;

- velcroid
  someone who sticks close to a celebrity during a photo opportunity.

| # Having fun with words

Another large collection of new words dances on the very edge of usefulness: they are entertaining, even amusing (at least to some), but it's hard to say that the language would be much the poorer if they hadn't been invented. They are often to be found in journalistic writing. Here are some examples:

- **tankini**
  a tank top worn with a bikini bottom;

- **chatterati**
  where the chattering classes and the so-called literati meet: TV personalities and chat-show hosts, newspaper columnists, and other luminaries;

- **evangineer**
  someone who has the evangelistic urge to change the world and the technological skill with which to do it;

- **paperazzi**
  (No, not a misprint!) The reporters from tabloid newspapers who chase after celebrities in the same way as their photographer colleagues the paparazzi do.

Getting your bearings

As we have seen, the problem with this mass of new words is that many of them soon disappear. True, there is a need for some of them, but there is also a large element of fashion. This means not only that fashionable words will soon be dropped and disappear, but also that using them, even when they are still fashionable, can irritate some people. So an unthinking and enthusiastic adoption of all the new words you encounter is probably not a good idea. By all means be alert to them; this is one way of being aware of changes in the thinking and lifestyles of the people around you. But be as wary of new words as you are of jargon—and before you use them, make sure that you know exactly what they mean and how they are used!

Bushisms

An example of the problems that can occur when people don't have a proper grasp of the words they use is provided by President George W. Bush, whose misadventures with the English language are well known. Sometimes he just picks the wrong word:

> I am a person who recognizes the fallacy of humans.

> A tax cut is really one of the anecdotes to coming out of an economic illness.

At others he misses the right word and uses a near approximation to it:

> They said, 'You know, this issue doesn't seem to resignate with the people....'

> They misunderestimated me.

To sum up ...

1 The rapid extension of popular culture and global communication has led to an explosion of new words.

2 In some cases words are coined to satisfy a long-felt need.

3 More frequently, a new concept and the word used to express it arrive at more or less the same time.

4 Many new words are devised not just to express a new concept but also to make a serious or playful comment on it.

5 Other words are created mainly for entertainment or pleasure.

6 A large number of the new words that are coined will not survive for long. They are subject to fashion and so only have a short life.

8 | The grammar of words

If you are one of the many readers who have a deep suspicion of the word 'grammar', don't be put off by the title of this chapter. As far as possible it avoids detailed analysis of sentences and it uses very little technical terminology. There is a more detailed examination of the subject matter in Part B. But the fact remains that it is difficult to talk about words without having some basic understanding of how sentences work, and of a few of the terms used to describe parts of a sentence and different kinds of word.

We use words to construct the sentences with which we communicate what we want to say. We can divide words into two main sorts:

- the words that carry a meaning that we can explain;

- the 'little' words with which we glue the meaning together.

The first sort are the words you look up in a dictionary if you want to check their meaning. Words like:

cabbage   unremarkable   terrify   concentrically

The others are words that you would not normally look up in a dictionary, although they can be found there:

because   under   herself   the

This chapter focuses on the first group of words. It looks at word classes—how words are used in sentences—and word structure—how words are built up.

Word classes

The words we shall look at fall into four classes: nouns, adjectives, verbs, and adverbs.

Nouns

These are words we use to refer to people, places, things and ideas:

Nouns are explained
in more detail on
page 86.

farmer   mountain   book   success

Nouns are sometimes used on their own in a sentence, but more often they combine with other words to make a **noun phrase**:

a worried **farmer**

her remarkable **success**

In each case the words we have added before and after the noun answer the question 'What kind of…?' So, 'What kind of farmer?' Answer: 'a worried farmer'.

Adjectives

One of the commonest ways of answering the question 'What kind of…?' is to use an adjective. Many adjectives tell us about the qualities of things:

Adjectives are
explained in more
detail on page 87.

peculiar   extensive   green   lumpy

Others place things into categories:

nuclear   annual   pregnant   unique

As we have seen, adjectives often combine with nouns in noun phrases. They are also used after verbs like 'be':

The result of the poll was **disastrous**.

Verbs are explained in more detail on pages 88–9.

Verbs

The grammatical term 'verb' has two distinct but related meanings:

■ a class of words, like 'noun' and 'adjective';

■ a part of a sentence, like 'subject' and 'object'.

In the first sense, a verb is a single word, like *ran, should,* and *fetch.* In the second sense it may be one word or a group of words. In the examples that follow the verb is printed in bold.

> The train **was** usually late.
> She **was washing** her car.
> Peter **should have been writing** a letter.

Verbs are words that refer to actions (like 'run') or states (like 'dream'), or that link two halves of a sentence together (like 'am' in the sentence 'I am happy').

Adverbs

We saw how adjectives add information to a noun or to the subject of a sentence. Adverbs also add information, often to the sentence as a whole. In the sample sentences that follow, the adverbs are printed in bold type:

> We'll **soon** be there.
> The thief ran **away**.
> She walked **slowly** down the road.

Many adverbs answer one of three questions: when? ('soon'), where? ('away'), how? ('slowly'). As you can see from the examples, adverbs often work quite closely with the verb—hence their name.

Word structure

Long words that you've never seen before need not be a problem—if you have the tools for analysing them. If you know how
to break long words into their separate parts, then you stand a
good chance of being able to work out what they mean.

Word families

Some groups of words go naturally together because of their
structure. If you look at the list of words in the box, it isn't difficult to pick out one group of words with strong family ties:

contented	unhappiness
happy	unhappily
serene	unhappier
ecstatic	smiling
happily	joyful
happiness	unhappiest
placid	smug
unhappy	happier
excited	happiest

happy
happily
happiness
unhappy
unhappiness
unhappily
unhappier
unhappiest
happier
happiest

*All happy families
resemble one
another, each
unhappy family
is unhappy in
its own way.*

Leo Tolstoy, *Anna Karenina*

It isn't too difficult to see why our eyes naturally group those words together: they are all related to the word 'happy'. We could draw out the family tree of 'happy' like this:

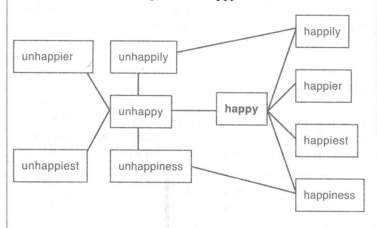

Affixes

If you look at the diagram above you can see that various 'bits' have been added to the front and to the end of a base word 'happy'. English spelling changes the spelling of the base word in order to accommodate the ending, removing the 'y' and replacing it with an 'i'. The 'bits' at the beginning and the end are called affixes. Those that come before the base are prefixes and those that come after are suffixes:

Prefix	Base	Suffix
un	happi	ly
		er
		est
		ness

Prefixes

The commonest prefixes are listed in the table on pages 96–7.

As the name suggests, prefixes are 'fix'ed at the beginning ('pre') of the word. Almost all prefixes add to, subtract from, or change in some other way the meaning of the base word. So we can turn 'happy' into its opposite by adding the prefix -un: 'unhappy'.

Suffixes

Suffixes come after the base word. They do not alter its meaning, but change the way in which it can be used. By adding a suffix, we can change a verb into a noun, for example, or an adjective into an adverb.

There is a more detailed explanation of this on pages 98–9.

To sum up ...

1 We can look at words from two points of view:
   ○ how we use them in sentences;
   ○ how they are constructed.

2 Nouns are words that we use to refer to people, places, things, and ideas. They are sometimes used on their own, but more often combine with words like adjectives to make noun phrases.

3 Adjectives are used to provide more information about people, places, things, and ideas in noun phrases. They are also used in sentences after verbs like 'is' to provide more information about the subject.

4 Verbs refer to actions or states or are used to link two halves of the sentence together. They change their form according to their use within a sentence.

5 Adverbs provide more information about the whole sentence and are often closely linked to the verb.

6 It is useful to be able to break long words down into their constituent parts.

7 All words have a stem, the main part of the word. In addition there are parts which come before or after the stem. These are called affixes.

8 Affixes which come before the stem are called prefixes. They add to or change the meaning of the stem in some way.

9 Affixes which come after the stem are called suffixes. They change the stem into a new word, often one which belongs to a different word class. So, for example, we can change and adjective into an adverb by adding the letters '-ly'.

9 | Getting a grip on words

Ten-point plan

You are almost at the end of Part A. Part B is for reference. So now is a good time to take stock of what you have read and to develop an action plan. Much of what you have read in the preceding chapters can be boiled down into a ten-point plan:

1 **Take a positive attitude towards building your vocabulary.**
Remember that you have a passive vocabulary of words that you understand but rarely or never use. There are also a lot of words that you have seen or heard more than once but feel rather hazy about. Make a real effort to move words from these lists into the list of words that you feel comfortable about using.

2 **Use a good dictionary and thesaurus.**
If you need to find out or check the meanings of words, use a good dictionary. Work at it to make sure that you can use it efficiently and confidently. When writing, make use of a good thesaurus to find all the possible words and then to choose the best for your purpose.

3 **Remember that there is always a choice of words.**
Especially when writing, don't just settle for the first word that comes into your head. Think of other words that might be more accurate or more suitable. Whenever possible use a thesaurus to widen the choice of words available to you.

4 **Think about your audience's skills and knowledge.**
We use words to communicate, and communication is a two-way process. Think about who will hear or read your words—

make an assessment of their language skills and try to avoid words that they will find difficult or impossible to understand. Think also of their knowledge of the subject you are talking or writing about. Use terms that they will understand and, if you have to use a term that they may not be familiar with, make sure that you explain it the first time you use it.

5 **Think about the social setting in which you are communicating.**
Communication isn't just about using language accurately; it also involves thinking about your relationship with your audience. Words that are fine in one social setting will jar horribly in another. So think about formality and informality. By all means use colloquial language and even slang in the right context, but if you are unsure of your audience, avoid slang like the plague.

6 **Avoid jargon.**
Jargon is fun for insiders but can be guaranteed to irritate everyone else. So unless you are in the company of 'consent ing adults in private', don't use it!

7 **Tune into new words but don't be seduced by them.**
Language is a living organism and words grow old and die, just as new words are born. English is a world language. It is par excellence the language of the Internet. So new words come flooding into it from all over the globe. Some of these will become a part of the language and will be widely used. Most will soon fade and die. So be aware of new words, cherish them, but don't waste time trying to be always in fashion. If you do, you will probably end up looking ridiculous.

8 **Learn more about how words are used in sentences.**
You cannot develop your vocabulary or use dictionaries and other word reference books effectively unless you have a basic knowledge of how words work in sentences. This will also benefit your use of the langauge as a whole, especially your writing.

9 **Understand word structure and use your knowledge to tackle new words.**

Many words are constructed from common parts. Work to understand this system: learn the meanings of common prefixes and the uses of suffixes in the building of new words. Use this knowledge to help with any long words that bother you.

10 **Have fun with words!**

The English language is a wonderful thing: infinitely expressive, remarkably flexible, and growing in scope all the time. So don't let words master you—get a grip on them. And enjoy them.

A few quotations to speed you on your way

■ All books are either dreams or swords,
You can cut, or you can drug, with words. (Amy Lowell)

■ Be not the slave of words. (Thomas Carlyle)

■ In prose, the worst thing one can do with words is surrender to them. (George Orwell)

■ We must use words as they are used or stand aside from life. (Ivy Compton-Burnett)

■ Let thy speech be short, comprehending much in few words. (Ecclesiasticus)

■ *Et semel emissum volat irrevocabile verbum*
Once a word has been uttered it flies free and cannot be recalled. (Horace)

■ Words are, of course, the most powerful drug used by mankind. (Rudyard Kipling)

■ Words are wise men's counters, they do but reckon with them, but they are the money of fools. (Thomas Hobbes)

Part B: Reference section
Contents

Word classes

Nouns

These are words we use to refer to people, places, things, and ideas. Most nouns:

- have singular and plural forms
  tree/trees
  child/children

- can be used as the subject of a sentence, either on their own, or preceded by 'a', 'an', or 'the'
  Cats make good pets.

- can be preceded by an adjective
  That's an **attractive cat**.

Nouns can be divided into groups according to use and meaning. The commonest arrangements are:

- **proper nouns and common nouns**
  Proper nouns are the names of people, places, and things that are unique. For example: 'Shakespeare', 'Parliament', 'Oxford'. As in these examples, the main words of proper nouns are written with initial capital letters. All other nouns are called common nouns.

- **countable and uncountable nouns**
  Most nouns have singular and plural forms: 'one cow', 'two cows'. A fairly small number of nouns refer to things that cannot be counted and so rarely if ever have a plural form. Examples are 'mud', 'milk', 'happiness'.

- **abstract and concrete nouns**
  Concrete nouns are those which refer to people, places, and things that can be experienced using the five senses.

For example: 'table', 'ice', 'wind'. Abstract nouns refer to things that exist in the mind alone. For example: 'beauty', 'fear', 'happiness'. It is sometimes argued that we should avoid the use of too many abstract nouns because they are remote from personal experience, but, as can be seen from the examples, they include many quite simple words that are very useful.

Adjectives

Adjectives refer to the qualities of people things and ideas, or help us to classify them:

We had a long, slow journey to Victoria.
The awards ceremony is an annual event.

Adjectives are used in two main ways:

- to modify nouns
  They usually come before the noun they modify:
  a **long**, **slow** journey
  This use of adjectives is called **attributive**.

- after verbs like 'be' and 'seem'
  The journey was **slow**.
  She seems **happy**.
  This use of adjectives is called **predicative**.

Most adjectives can be used in either of these two ways, but a few can only be used attributively (e.g. 'sole'). There is another small group that can only be used predicatively (e.g. 'alone').

Adjectives have absolute, comparative and superlative forms;

Absolute	Comparative	Superlative
fast	faster	fastest
good	better	best
wonderful	more wonderful	most wonderful

They can also be graded, by placing adverbs like 'fairly', 'very', and 'rather' in front of them:

a **fairly** interesting programme, a **rather** interesting programme,
a **very** interesting programme

Verbs

The grammatical term 'verb' has two distinct but related meanings:

■ a class of words, like 'noun' and 'adjective';

■ a part of a sentence, like 'subject' and 'object'.

In the first sense, a verb is a single word, like *ran, should, and fetch*. In the second sense it may be one word or a group of words. In the examples that follow the verb is printed in bold.

> The train **was** usually late.
> She **was washing** her car.
> Peter **should have been writing** a letter.

Some of us learned at school that verbs were 'doing words'. As adults we need a rather more comprehensive definition.

1. Verbs are words that refer to actions (like 'run') or states (like 'dream'), or that serve to link two halves of a sentence together (like 'am' in the sentence 'I am happy').

2. Verbs inflect: they change their form according to their use within a sentence. Regular verbs inflect like this:
   Stem: hope
   Present tense: I hope, she hopes
   Past tense: I hoped
   Present participle: hoping
   Past participle: hoped
   In regular verbs, like 'hope', the past tense and the past participle are the same, but some irregular verbs show a range of differences:

Stem:	swim	put	go	be
Past tense:	swam	put	went	was/were
Past participle:	swum	put	gone	been

3 Verbs can be divided into main verbs and auxiliary verbs. Main verbs can stand alone in a sentence:
   The dog ran away.
   Auxiliary verbs are used with main verbs, but do not normally

stand alone in a sentence:

Peter should have been writing a letter.

The auxiliary verbs are:

am is are was were be being been
has have had having
can could may might
will shall would should
must ought (to)

4. Main verbs can be divided into transitive and intransitive.
   Transitive verbs are those which are followed by an object:

   The dog bit the postman.

   Intransitive verbs are not followed by an object:

   The dog escaped.

| # Adverbs

Of all the word classes, adverbs are the most difficult to pin down satisfactorily. As we have seen, they can modify the meaning of adjectives:

It was a **fairly** interesting programme.

They can a similar thing with other adverbs:

The car was travelling **extremely** fast.

More often, however, adverbs add additional information to the sentence as a whole, or to its verb:

The car was travelling **fast**.
Fortunately the driver was skilful.

Meaning

Another way of thinking about adverbs is to consider the types of question they answer:

■ When?
We'll soon be there.

■ Where?
We'll soon be there.

■ How?
I walked slowly away.

Pronouns

As the name suggests, pronouns stand in for nouns. They enable us to avoid repeating nouns:

Peter says that he hasn't seen his sister recently.

But they can also help us avoid other kinds of repetition and wordiness, as is illustrated by these sentences:

The year 2000 was not a good one for the Brown family. It[1] was particularly disappointing for James Brown, who[2] was made redundant. This[3] came as a bolt from the blue.

1   This personal pronoun refers to the phrase 'the year 2000'.

2   This is a relative pronoun which links 'James Brown' to the clause describing him 'he lost his job' (see below).

3   This demonstrative pronoun refers to the fact that James Brown lost his job.

So pronouns can refer to nouns, noun phrases, and whole sentences and ideas, as well as introducing relative clauses.

Types of pronoun

Personal pronouns

I/me, you, he/him, she/her, it, we/us, they/them

Possessive

These are of two types: possessive pronouns and possessive determiners. Possessive pronouns can stand on their own in a sentence:

That's not your book, it's mine.

The possessive pronouns are: 'mine', 'his', 'hers', 'ours', 'yours', 'theirs'.

Possessive determiners come before a noun:

That's not your book, it's mine.

The possessive determiners are: my, his, her, our, your, their.

Reflexive pronoun

myself, himself, etc.

Demonstrative pronoun

this, that, these, those

Indefinite pronoun

some, someone, somebody, something
any, anyone, etc
none, no one, etc
everyone, etc

Interrogative pronouns

These are used to introduce certain types of question:
Who is that woman who is standing by the window?
They are: who, whom, what, whose, which

Relative pronouns

These introduce relative clauses:
Who is that woman **who** is standing by the window?
They are: who, whom, that, whose, which

Conjunctions

Conjunctions are an important 'glue' used to stick sentence elements together. They are conveniently divided into two groups.

Co-ordinating conjunctions

The commonest of these are:

> and, or, but

They can be used to join words:

> John **and** Mary

phrases:

> The Prime Minister **or** his Deputy

clauses:

> She bought several Lottery tickets, **but** she never won anything.

Subordinating conjunctions

This is a much larger group of words. As their name suggests they join two elements of a sentence of which one is more important than the other. Common subordinating conjunctions are:

after	although	as	because
before	if	since	so
unless	until	when	where
while			

Prepositions

Prepositions are another small group of small words. They are placed before a noun:

for teachers, **under** water

or before a noun phrase:

after my first drink
in alphabetical order

Common prepositions include:

about	above	across	after
against	along	among	around
as	at	before	behind
below	beneath	beside	between
beyond	but	by	despite
during	except	for	from
in	inside	into	less
like	near	of	off
on	onto*	over	past
round	since	through	throughout
till	to	towards	under
underneath	until	up	upon
with	within	without	

* Some people prefer to write this as two words: 'on to'.

Determiners

We have seen that adjectives normally come before the noun they refer to, forming noun phrases:

intelligent students
black cats

Determiners are words that come at the beginning of a noun phrase, before any adjectives that refer to the noun:

some intelligent students
the black cats

Common determiners are:

a	all	an	both
any	few	half	her
his	its	last	little
many	much	my	next
no	other	our	second
some	such	tenth	that
the	their	these	this
those	three	two	your

Of these the commonest by far are the articles: 'a/an', 'the'.

Prefixes

As the name suggests, prefixes are 'fix'ed at the beginning ('pre') of the word. Almost all prefixes add to, subtract from, or change in some other way the meaning of the base word. The commonest prefixes are listed in the table that follows, together with meanings and examples.

Prefix	Meaning	Example
a-	not, not affected by	amoral
ante-	before	antecedent
anti-	against	anti-pollution
arch-	chief	archpriest
auto-	self	autobiography
bi-	two	bipartisan
bio-	(from 'biology')	biodiversity
circum-	around	circumnavigate
co-	joint, together	cooperate
contra-	opposite	contradiction
counter-	against	counteract
crypto-	hidden	crypto-fascist
de-	making the opposite of	demystify
demi-	half	demigod
di-	two	dialogue
dis-	making the opposite of	disagree
du-/duo-	two	duotone
eco-	(from ecology)	eco-tourism
Euro-	(from European)	Eurodollar
ex-	former	ex-husband
	out of	export
fore-	in the front of, ahead of	forerunner
hyper-	very big	hypermarket
in-	not, opposite of	inexact
	in, into	insert

Prefix	Meaning	Example
inter-	between	inter-state
intra-	inside	intravenous
mal-	badly	maladministration
mega-	very large	megastar
mid-	middle	midlife
midi-	medium-sized	midi-length
mini-	small	minimarket
mis-	wrong, false	misadventure
mono-	one	monolingual
multi-	many	multi-layered
neo-	new	neolithic
non-	not, opposite of	non-partisan
out-	beyond	outreach
over-	too much	overreach
para-	ancillary	paramedic
	beyond	paranormal
poly-	many	polytonal
post-	after	post-election
pre-	before	pre-election
pro-	for	pro-gun
	deputy	proconsul
pseudo-	false	pseudo-intellectual
re-	again	rerun
	back	reverse
retro-	backwards	retrograde
self-	self	self-sufficient
semi-	half	semi-serious
sub-	below	sub-zero
super-	more than, special	superhuman
supra-	above	suprasensuous
sur-	more than, beyond	surreal
tele-	at a distance	television
trans-	across	trans-Siberian
tri-	three	tricycle
ultra-	beyond	ultraviolet
	very much indeed	ultra-careful
un-	not, opposite of	unnecessary
under-	below, less than	underachieve
uni-	one	unisex
vice-	deputy	vice-chancellor

Suffixes

Suffixes come after the base word. They do not alter its meaning, but change the way in which it can be used. By adding a suffix, we can change a verb into a noun, for example:

direct → director

and that noun into another noun:

director → directorship

Suffixes for making verbs

Suffix	Example	Original word class
-ify	beautify	VERB
-ise/-ize	idolize	VERB

Suffixes for making adjectives

Suffix	Example	Original word class
-able/-ible	excitable	VERB
-al/-ial	adverbial	NOUN
-ed	flat-roofed	NOUN
-esque	picturesque	NOUN
-ful	fateful	NOUN
-is	Icelandic	NOUN
-ical	economical	NOUN
-ish	childish	NOUN
-ive	possessive	VERB
-less	childless	NOUN

Suffix	Example	Original word class
-like	blood-like	NOUN
-ous	analagous	NOUN
-y	dozy	NOUN

Suffixes for making adverbs

Suffix	Example	Original word class
-ly	happily	ADJECTIVE
-wards	westwards	ADJECTIVE
-wise	clockwise	NOUN

Suffixes for making nouns

Suffix	Example	Original word class
-age	acreage	NOUN
-al	referral	VERB
-ant/-ent	inhabitant	VERB
-ation/-ion	examination	VERB
-dom	kingdom	NOUN
-ee	addressee	VERB
-eer	auctioneer	VERB
-er	abstainer	VERB
-ess	tigress	NOUN
-ery	slavery	NOUN
-ette	leatherette	NOUN
-ful	handful	NOUN
-hood	neighbourhood	NOUN
-ing	mooring	VERB
-ism	impressionism	NOUN
-ist	artist	NOUN
-ity	chastity	ADJECTIVE
-ment	postponement	VERB
-ness	happiness	ADJECTIVE
-ocracy	meritocracy	NOUN
-or	escalator	VERB
-ship	directorship	NOUN
-ster	mobster	NOUN

Confusables

This section contains some of the commonest groups of words that are sometimes confused. It does not include words that are confused because of their spelling (like 'curb' and 'kerb').

ability/capacity

Strictly speaking, an ability is a skill that you have gained, through practice, study, or in some other way. Capacity refers to a talent you were born with. 'Her *ability* at swimming and hockey is very commendable. Unfortunately she lacks the *capacity* to concentrate.' This distinction is, however, often ignored.

abnormal/subnormal

If something is abnormal it is outside the range of normal events. If a thing is subnormal it is below the normal level. So if a person is of subnormal intelligence their intelligence is below the average; if they are abnormally intelligent, their intelligence is extraordinary (usually extraordinarily high). 'Although he was of *subnormal* height his strength was *abnormal*.'

actuate/activate

If something actuates you it provides you with your drive or motivation. So we can say, 'His habits of hard work were *actuated* by fear of poverty'. To activate something is to make it active: 'The burglar alarm was *activated* by a movement in the kitchen.'

adduce/deduce

If you are making a case, or presenting an argument, you can adduce evidence to support it. When you read or hear something you may use reasoning to deduce other information or ideas from it. 'To prove her argument of negligence, she *adduced* the rapid and uncontrolled spread of the disease. I *deduced* from the way she spoke that she was still angry about it.'

adherence/adhesion

Adherence means holding to or supporting a belief or opinion. Adhesion refers to the physical sticking of one thing to another. 'The *adhesion* of human skin to very cold metal is well known—as is my *adherence* to the belief that one should always wear gloves for jobs like this.'

affect/effect

These two are sometimes confused. If something affects you, it has an effect on you. To effect something, on the other hand, is to make it happen: 'The criminals effected entry through a skylight, but their enthusiasm for continuing was *affected* by the fierce barking of a dog inside one of the bedrooms'.

affront/effrontery

An affront is an insult. Effrontery is impudence: 'She had the *effrontery* to correct my grammar! I took it as an *affront* to my reputation as a teacher.'

amoral/immoral

If a someone or something is amoral, they are without a set of moral values. So, for example, babies are amoral, as are many works of art. If a person or action is immoral, then they are breaking the moral code. 'The novel depicted an *amoral* society where anything went. I knew from personal experience that the writer was an *immoral* person.'

apprehend/comprehend

If you apprehend an idea you have grasped it in your mind. This meaning is also carried by comprehend with the added meaning of 'understand'. (So someone may apprehend an idea without yet fully comprehending it.) 'The MP *apprehended* the beliefs of the protestors but was far from *comprehending* their motives.'

astrology/astronomy

Astronomy is the scientific study of heavenly bodies. Astrology uses the stars to foretell people's futures.

bail/bale

A bale is a bundle of something, such a straw or paper. In British English it is also used as a verb: you bale water from a boat and you can bale out of an aeroplane. (In American

English, this verb is spelled 'bail'.) Bails are used in cricket, and someone who is arrested by the police is often allowed to go home on bail.

bathos/pathos

Bathos means 'anti-climax'. If something has pathos it inspires pity.

between/among/through

These three prepositions are sometimes misused. You use 'between' to refer to something that stands or moves with things on either side of it: 'The route passed between two brick pillars.' 'Among' implies that something is in or moves through the middle of a group of scattered items: 'She knew that she was among friends.' 'Through' implies a movement which actually enters something and exits from it. So to say that 'The route passed through two brick pillars' suggests that it was necessary to penetrate solid brick. It is correctly used in sentences such as: 'A shiver of excitement passed through the audience.'

capital/corporal

Capital punishment is the death penalty; corporal punishment means physical punishment, such as beating,

childish/childlike

Both words refer to behaviour that is appropriate to a child. 'Childlike' is an emotionally neutral term, implying neither praise nor blame. 'Childish', on the other hand, implies that the person concerned was old enough to have known better.

climactic/climatic/climacteric

'Climactic' is the adjective that comes from 'climax', while climatic comes from 'climate'. 'Climacteric' is a noun and an adjective referring to a critical point or stage in a person's life.

collage/montage

These two words are often taken to mean the same thing, but they do have slightly different meanings. Anything which involves superimposing two or more items on top of each other to make a composite whole can be called a montage—whether the things are physical, like photographs, or computer images. If the things superimposed are stuck onto a base with glue, then the whole is properly a collage, from the French for 'glue'.

commissionaire/commissioner

A commissioner is a person who has been made a member or head of a team who have been assigned a particular duty (e.g. the Metropolitan Police Commissioner). A commissionaire is a uniformed doorman.

complaisant/complacent

A complacent person is self-satisfied. If someone is complaisant they accept a situation and are willing to go along with it (e.g. a complaisant lover is aware of being two-timed, and condones or even supports the situation). 'Arthur Jones was fat, ugly, and *complacent*, which explained why his wife was *complaisant* when he ran off with the barmaid from the "Jolly Fisherman".'

compliment/complement

If you pay someone a compliment, you commend them on something. A complement is what makes something complete, so a ship's complement is its crew. If something is described in a sales catalogue as 'complimentary', it means that it is free; if it is complementary, you probably need it as well as the item you have ordered, and you will have to pay for it.

compose/compile

To compose a letter or piece of music means to make it up. To compile a list, for example, is to bring together the different elements required for a particular purpose. 'Wengstein *compiled* a detailed list of all the piano sonatas she had *composed*.'

comprise/consist/compose

These three words have related meanings and can cause minor problems. Whereas 'comprise' is a straightforward verb taking an object, the other two verbs are normally followed by a preposition:

The team comprises nine English players and two Italians.
The team consists of nine English players and two Italians.
The team is composed of nine English players and two Italians.

compulsive/compulsory

If an activity is compulsive, you may find it difficult or impossible to give it up: 'Arthur is a compulsive liar.' If it is compulsory, then you are obliged by law or by some other external authority to do it: 'Students are reminded that attendance at lectures is compulsory.'

consistently/persistently

Both adverbs refer to actions that are repeated and predictably so. 'Consistently' merely records the facts; 'persistently' states or implies that the repetition is deliberate:
'The train I catch to work has been consistently late this week.'
'The ticket collector is persistently rude to passengers.'

contagious/infectious

If a disease is contagious, it is transmitted by physical contact. An infectious disease can be communicated through bacteria in the air or in water.

contiguous/contagious

A contagious disease is one spread by physical contact. If two objects are contiguous they are touching.

continual/continuous

Something that is continuous goes on without interruption. If it is continual it keeps on happening. 'There were continual interruptions to the match because of rain. During the evening the rain became continuous.'

councillor/counsellor

A councillor is a member of a council; a counsellor is someone who provides advice. (In American English a counsellor is a barrister.) 'She stopped being a district councillor when she became a marriage guidance counsellor.'

credence/credibility

If you believe something to be true you can be said to give it credence. The features that make something believable give it credibility. 'The story lacked credibility, even though some people gave it credence.'

credible/credulous

Something that is credible is believable. A person who is credulous is very willing to believe things. 'Although he was generally rather credulous he felt her story lacked any kind of credibility.'

deceitful/deceptive

People are deceitful when they set out to deceive (and they perform deceitful actions). Something that is deceptive can easily deceive you, but there isn't necessarily any intention involved. It is easy to misinterpret a deceptive situation, but this does not necessarily mean that anyone has been deceitful.

defective/deficient

Something that is defective has got something wrong with it. Something that is deficient is lacking something. So a machine may be defective because it is deficient, lacking a vital part, but it cannot be deficient because it is defective. 'I examined my new mountain bike and found that it was deficient: the front wheel was missing three spokes. So I complained to the shop that they had sold me defective goods.'

delusion/illusion

Both words refer to an impression that something is true when it isn't. An illusion, however, is either already known to be false or will be at some point be thus known in the future. A delusion is an illusion that someone holds to in the face of all reason. If someone has delusions, they believe things to be true that other people realize are illusions.

deprecate/depreciate

If you deprecate something you show disapproval of it. If something depreciates its value falls. If you depreciate something you make it clear that you think little of it. This meaning is quite close to that of 'deprecate', which is why the two are sometimes confused. 'Deprecate', however, is stronger and implies more emotional involvement.

discreet/discrete

'Discreet' is used to refer to a person who can keep a secret. 'Discrete' means separate and distinct.

discrepancy/disparity

Disparity means inequality between two things. If you compare two lists or sets of figures and notice a discrepancy, it means that something which occurs in one and should also occur in the other, doesn't.

dispose of/dispense with

If you dispose of something, you throw it away; if you dispense with it, you do without it.

dominate/domineer

Both words mean to be in control of or to have considerable power over people and situations. Dominate is neutral in tone, however, whereas domineer is critical and implies that the person involved is behaving like a tyrant. 'In public Miriam was a *dominating* character and many people thought her larger than life. Her husband was rather feeble, despite trying to be *domineering* at home.'

effective/effectual/efficient/efficacious

If something is effective it has the desired effect. The same can be said of people: 'She was a very effective minister.' 'Effectual' applies to actions not to people and means 'having the effect of': 'Her period as Prime Minister spelled the effectual end of investment in the railways.' Something is efficient if it achieves results promptly and economically, and the adjective can also be applied to people. Only things can be efficacious—when they have the desired effect (e.g. 'The most efficacious remedy for the common cold is to let nature take its course').

emigrant/immigrant/migrant

Migrants are people or other creatures that move from one territory to another. Immigrants are those coming into a territory; emigrants are those departing from a territory.

empathy/sympathy

If you have sympathy for someone, then you have fellow-feeling for them. Empathy is the ability to imagine yourself in their position.

endemic/epidemic/pandemic

All refer to diseases. If a disease is endemic it is common in an area or population and people are likely to be exposed to it. An epidemic refers to a widespread occurrence of a disease in a region. A pandemic is an epidemic that is even more widespread.

envy/envious/jealousy/jealous

Envy is a longing for something that belongs to someone else. Jealousy is the consuming emotion that you do not trust another person to be faithful to you. It can also mean that you are determined to guard your own belongings or rights.

epigram/epigraph/epitaph/epilogue/epithet

An epigram is a witty saying or 'bon mot'. An epigraph is a carved inscription or a short printed statement at the beginning of a book. An epitaph is a carved memorial statement about someone who has died—either on their grave, or elsewhere such as in a church. The epilogue to a book or play is a short section at the end, and an epithet is an adjective, or descriptive expression. (The word is also used to refer to an expression of abuse.)

equable/equitable

An equable person is easy-going; an equitable settlement is fair to both sides. 'Although the final divorce settlement was far from *equitable*, James didn't seem to mind—he was a very *equable* person.'

exalt/exult

If you exalt someone or something you raise them up. To exult is to rejoice. 'The High Priest *exalted* the new-born prince and the whole crowd *exulted*.'

expedient/expeditious

If a thing is expedient it is convenient or advantageous; if it is expeditious it is speedy. 'Time is short, so I should find it very expedient if you would seek an expeditious solution to this problem.'

explicit/implicit

'Explicit' means stated directly; 'implicit' means stated indirectly. 'His hostility was implicit in his tone of voice; explicitly, in what he said, he was very polite.'

factious/fractious

A group that is factious is likely to split into smaller groups; a person or group that is fractious is argumentative or quarrelsome.

factitious/fictitious

While 'factitious' means artificially achieved, 'fictitious' means invented. So a politician might generate a factitious body of opinion in favour of something by spreading rumours—but the body of opinion would then really exist. If the politician referred to a fictitious body of opinion, it would not exist, but would be made up.

fewer/less/fewest/least

Few, fewer, and fewest should be used with nouns that can have a plural ('countable' or 'count' nouns). 'Less' and 'least' should be used with nouns that cannot be counted ('uncountable' or 'noncount' nouns). So it should be 'fewer drinks', but 'less water'.

flaunt/flout

To flaunt something is to show it off in a shameless or outrageous way ('She was going round flaunting her new fiancée—even before the divorce was through'). To flout is deliberately to ignore a rule or accepted standard ('By behaving in this way she was flouting the islanders' normal codes of behaviour').

gesticulate/gesture

A person who gesticulates waves their arms about, probably fairly wildly. A gesture is a more restrained action, usually with a meaning.

glance/glimpse

To glance is to take a quick look. To glimpse is to get a brief sight of something.

gourmet/gourmand

A gourmet is an expert in the appreciation of fine food and wine, a connoisseur. A gourmand, when sitting down to a meal, is more interested in quantity than quality.

graceful/gracious

Graceful describes a person's attractive bearing and ease of movement. Gracious implies kindness or courtesy from a superior, and can sound condescending.

homogeneous/homogenous

'Homogeneous' means 'of the same kind'. The stress falls on the third syllable. 'Homogenous' means 'having a common descent or origin'. The stress is on the second syllable.

illegible/unreadable

If something is illegible, it is impossible to read because it is badly written or printed. If a text is unreadable, readers give up, because it is not to their taste, is badly composed, is too difficult to understand, or for some other reason.

imbue/infuse/instil

While you can say that something imbued a person with a quality ('The experience imbued David with a sense of purpose'), you cannot say that it imbued the quality into the person. For that you need 'infuse' or 'instil' ('The experience instilled a sense of purpose into David').

immunity/impunity

Foreign diplomats enjoy immunity from prosecution. In this sense immunity means 'exemption'. A second meaning is the medical one whereby inoculation, for example, will protect the patient by producing immunity from certain diseases. Impunity is freedom from any unpleasant consequences of your actions. 'The diplomatic *immunity* enjoyed by staff at the embassy meant that they could park where they liked with *impunity*.'

imply/infer

In the past these two words were used with similar meanings—by Jane Austen, for example. Strict contemporary usage makes a distinction, although it is frequently ignored. If you imply something, you hint at it through the words you use, without stating it directly. Your audience can then infer it from your words.

inapt/inept

Both words are derived from the word apt. Inapt has the sense of 'inappropriate, unsuitable'. Inept means 'foolish, ineffectual'.

ingenious/ingenuous

Someone or something that is ingenious is clever, possibly in a fairly intricate way. Someone who is ingenuous, on the other hand, is naïve.

into/in to/onto/on to

'Into' indicates 'the intention of being inside': 'They drove into the town.' Separated as 'in to', the word to indicates the purpose of going in: 'The parent came in to see the headmaster.' 'Onto' is less well established as a single word and can well be written as two words. It is essential that the two words are used when 'on' means 'forward' or 'ahead' as in 'They drove on to the next town' or 'She went on to say that she was really sorry'. In speech, of course, we make the difference between the members of each pair clear through stress and intonation.

intolerable/intolerant

'Intolerable' means 'unbearable', 'impossible to put up with'. 'Intolerant' means 'unable to tolerate' and so possibly 'narrow-minded'.

intrude/obtrude/protrude

You intrude by forcing yourself or your opinions into the company or conversation of others. To obtrude is to push forward without good reason; the adjective 'obtrusive' means 'too noticeable'. To protrude is to stick out: 'We felt we had *intruded* on the estate agent's conversation with another customer, but we had to say that we found the pink paint on the front of the house *obtrusive*, and that an ugly conservatory *protruded* from the back.'

inveigh/inveigle

To inveigh against something is to protest strongly against it. To inveigle is to entice, to ensnare: 'He *inveighed* against the incompetence of a financial adviser who had *inveigled* him into putting his savings into shares just before the market crashed.'

judicial/judicious

'Judicial' applies to the administration of justice, the judicial process through courts of law. 'Judicious' means 'of sound judgement, sensible, discreet'.

lawful/legal/legitimate/licit

All four mean 'permitted by law' with different shades of meaning. 'Lawful' indicates 'entitlement' and therefore 'rightful' will often express the meaning. 'Legal' has the force of 'the law of the land' and also 'connected with the law' and in 'the legal profession'. 'Legitimate' means 'sanctioned by legal authority' and is applied particularly to children born to a married couple. It is used of a monarch's title which rests on hereditary right: 'our legitimate ruler'. 'Licit', which is rarely used, means 'not forbidden by law', 'permissible'. Its opposite, 'illicit', is far more common.

lay/lie

The confusion between these two verbs comes partly from the fact that both are irregular but have overlapping forms:

Present tense	Past tense	Past participle
I lie	I lay	I have lain
I lay	I laid	I have laid

So 'I lay' is the present tense of 'lay' and the past tense of 'lie'. The words have different meanings. 'To lie' never takes an object and means to put oneself into a recumbent position (as in 'to lie down') or to be in such a position. So, for example, we can say, 'She was lying on the ground.' 'To lay' must have an object and means to place something down; so, for examples, hens lay eggs. We also use the word to refer to arranging cutlery on a dining table: laying the table.

legible/readable

Legible applies to writing or print which is physically capable of being read. Readable applies to a text which can be read with some enjoyment. 'This book is highly *readable*, it's just a pity that the print isn't a bit more *legible*.'

libel/slander

Both words refer to defaming a person's character. Libel is written, or published in some other form; slander is spoken.

literate/literal/literary

A person who can read and write is literate. Literal means 'factually true'—so you cannot say 'It was literally raining cats and dogs'. A literary allusion would be a reference to something written about in a work of literature. 'Peter was a very *literal*-minded person, so my *literary* references left him cold. Sometimes it's difficult to believe he's even *literate*.'

loathe/loath/loth

To loathe something is to hate it. 'Loath' and 'loth' are different spellings of the same adjective expressing reluctance: 'I am loath/loth to disagree with you on this point, but I think you are wrong.'

meantime/meanwhile

The words convey the same meaning, although 'meantime' is commonly used as a noun and 'meanwhile' as an adverb. 'We have to wait for the Chairman, but meanwhile/in the mean-time perhaps we can discuss the staff party'

momentary/momentous

Momentary is 'lasting only a moment', 'brief'. Momentous is 'of great significance'.

nadir/zenith

Originally astronomical terms for the point in the skies directly below and above the observer, nadir and zenith are now used figuratively for 'low point' and 'high point' respectively, as in the following example: 'The general strike proved to be the *nadir* of the government's fortunes: its landslide victory at the general election had been the *zenith*.'

nearby/near by

As an adjective this word is spelt 'nearby': 'There are good shops in the nearby town.' As an adverb it can be spelt as one word or two: 'Some good friends live nearby/near by.' This construction is not used as a preposition: 'The town is near (not nearby) the Downs.'

passed/past

'Passed' is the past tense and past participle of the verb 'to pass'. 'We passed their house yesterday. We have passed it several times'. Past has several functions:
Adjective: during the **past** year
Adverb: The seagull glided **past**.
Noun: Let us put the **past** behind us.
Preposition: We drove **past** their house.

perpetrate/perpetuate

'Perpetrate' means 'to commit (something bad). 'Perpetrator' is often used to mean 'criminal'. To perpetuate is to cause something to continue: 'We formed a charitable trust to *perpetuate* his memory'.

perquisite/prerequisite

Informally shortened to 'perk', a perquisite is an extra benefit attached to some jobs. 'A valuable *perquisite* is free medical insurance.' A prerequisite is a condition which must be satisfied in advance. 'Rigorous training is a *prerequisite* for becoming a special constable.'

practical/practicable

'Practical' applied to a person means 'capable', 'sensible'. 'A practical proposition' is a scheme capable of being carried out, put into practice: the idea is practicable, so in some contexts the two words are virtually interchangeable. 'Practicable' suggests the possibility and practical the wisdom of a course of action: 'I know it's *practicable* to move our offices to Caithness, but is it *practical*?'

precede/proceed

'Precede' means to go first, to go in front. 'Proceed' means to go further, to carry on, to continue. 'The Lord Mayor was *preceded* by mounted police as he *proceeded* on his way through the town.'

precipitate/precipitous

A precipitate action would be sudden and possibly ill-advised. 'Precipitous' means very steep: 'a *precipitous* mountain crag'.

prescribe/proscribe

'Prescribe' is to recommend, to advise or specify. 'Proscribe' is to advise against, to prohibit. Spoken at speed, the words can sound the same. Since they are virtually opposites, it is important to make clear which one you mean.

prevaricate/procrastinate

To prevaricate is to speak evasively and deceitfully. 'Questioned by police he was tempted to prevaricate.' To procrastinate is to delay. 'As the proverb states: "Procrastination is the thief of time".'

principal/principle

As an adjective 'principal' means 'main', 'chief'. 'The *principal* speaker at the dinner was the Prime Minister'. As a noun it may mean the person at the head of an institution—the *principal* of the college. 'Principal', used as a noun, may also mean the leading performer in a play or opera, or the original sum of money, the capital, as opposed to the income derived from it. People who act 'according to their *principles*' are pursuing a personal code of conduct they have established.

psychiatry/psychology

Psychiatry is the treatment of mental disorders. Psychology is the study of the mind.

rare/scarce

'Rare' means 'uncommon', 'seldom seen'. 'Elephants are common in the game reserves of East Africa, but white rhinos are rare.' 'Rare' can also carry the sense of 'valuable'. 'Many rare paintings were destroyed in the fire.' 'Scarce' indicates a shortage of a particular commodity which may be plentiful elsewhere. 'Salt was scarce in the neighbouring country, so it was often smuggled in.' 'Rare', but not 'scarce', can mean 'infrequent'. 'Because they had been good, the children were given a rare treat.'

remittance/remission/remittal/remit

'Remittance' means payment which is to be sent for goods ordered. It does, however, include all possible forms of such a payment. It can seem a rather pretentious word. Remission provides relief from pain or disease, or from the guilt of sins. It is also the correct term for the legal shortening of a prison sentence. 'Remittal' is a legal term meaning the removal of a case to another court of justice. 'Remit' is the verb for all the preceding meanings:

We **remitted** the sum of six thousand pounds to your agents last week.

His sentence was **remitted** to community service.

The case was **remitted** to the High Court.

The word 'remit' is also used as a noun to mean 'area of responsibility'. 'The *remit* of this committee is to consider corruption in the sport.' In speech 'remit' as a noun has the stress on the first syllable.

shined/shone

Both words can be the past tense of 'shine'. 'Shined' is reserved for the meaning 'polished' ('I shined my shoes').

stalactites/stalagmites

In limestone caves stalactites hang down. Stalagmites stick up. The easiest way to remember is from the first of the two central consonants: the 'c' in the middle of stalactites stands for 'ceiling', while the 'g' in the middle of stalagmite stands for 'ground'.

temerity/timidity

'I don't know how you can have the *temerity* to hand in a scruffy piece of work like that,' says the teacher, and the pupil learns that 'temerity' means boldness and daring tinged with cheek. 'Timidity' applies to someone who is anxious, hesitant, and fearful.

transparent/translucent

Clear glass is transparent—you can see through it. The word is also used metaphorically, as in 'a transparent excuse'—one that you can see through. 'Translucent', while similar in meaning, emphasizes the idea of light passing through. (The word derives from Latin 'lux': light). So cut glass or frosted glass or the polythene product used in some greenhouses is not transparent but translucent.

trilogy/trio/trinity/triad

Three volumes of a literary work form a trilogy. A trio of three musicians may perform a trio composed for such a group. 'Trio' is also used more generally for a group of three people or things. The Trinity is the Christian 'three in one' of God the Father, Son, and Holy Spirit. 'Trinity' can be used as the second meaning of trio given above. 'Triad', still with the meaning 'three', is a specialist word with applications in music, chemistry, mathematics, and Welsh literature.

unconscious/subconscious

In Freudian psychology the subconscious is that part of the mind which lies just below the surface, of whose workings we are from time to time partially aware. The unconscious is deeper below the surface and we are never directly aware of it. In modern usage most people make little distinction between the two.

uneatable/inedible

If you find something uneatable, you think that it is not palatable to eat; if it is inedible it is impossible to eat it without great difficulty or even harm.

venal/venial

'Venal' means 'capable of being bought' and is now commonly applied to officials in positions which should have been conferred for merit and not for favours or money. 'Venial' means pardonable, and is applied to an error or fault which can be excused or overlooked.

Glossary

active vocabulary

The words that a person knows and is confident to use in speech and/or writing.

adjective

A class of words. Adjectives are normally used before nouns to add meaning: 'a large green door', or after a verb like 'be' to add meaning to the subject:

Subject	Verb	Adjective
The door	was	green.

Some adjectives, like 'alone', can only be used in this second way; others, like 'lone', can only be used in the first way.

adverb

A class of words. Adverbs frequently act upon the sentence as a whole, providing information about, for example, place, time, and manner. Examples are:

Place: here, away, somewhere
Time: soon, already, still
Manner: easily, fast, slowly

They can also be combined with adjectives to intensify them:
very easy, rather attractive
and in a similar way with adverbs:
extremely slowly, very fast

affix

A group of letters placed at the beginning (prefix) or the end (suffix) of a word.

audience

The person(s) to whom a spoken or written text is addressed. When we communicate we should be aware of our audience and select words accordingly.

compound conjunctions

Conjunctions that are used to link two words ('tired but happy'), two phrases ('the Prime Minister or the Foreign Secretary'), or two clauses ('She went out and did not return for three hours'). The two items linked by a compound conjunction are always of equal status in the sentence (i.e. one is not more important than the other).

compound word

A word made up of two other words, for example, 'deskbound', 'jack-knife', 'armchair'.

conjunction

A class of words. Conjunctions divide into compound and subordinating conjunctions.

connotations

Words have literal meanings (which you can find by looking them up in a dictionary). They also have connotations: they provide information about the writer's or speaker's attitude towards things. (When an estate agent describes the garden of a property as 'easily managed' it is intended to show it in a favourable light. Another person might call it 'cramped' or 'pathetically small'.)

consonant

A term that is used to describe letters and also the sounds of the language. The consonant letters are: b c d f g h j k l m n p q r s t v w x y z. Consonant sounds are those which require the speaker to block the passage of air from the lungs with the tongue, teeth, or some other part of the mouth (as opposed to vowel sounds, which are made with the mouth open and unblocked).

conversion

The process by which a word is moved from one word class to another. The word 'down', for example, is normally a preposition ('down the road') or an adverb ('I fell down'). We can, however, use it as verb: 'He downed the drink in one gulp.'

derivation

Information about the origins of a word, as provided by many dictionaries.

determiner

A class of words. Determiners come before the noun and also before any adjectives. The commonest are the articles 'a(n)' and 'the'. Others are possessives like 'my' and quantifiers like 'man'.

etymology

The origins of a word.

euphemism

A word or phrase used to avoid speaking directly of something that the speaker finds distasteful or embarrassing.

formal

Language that is intended for 'public consumption' and designed not to offend because of its lack or seriousness or respect (whether for the subject or the audience). It is language on its best behaviour, and contrasts with colloquial or informal language.

grammar

The study of the way in which words are combined into sentences.

headword

The main word or lead entry in a dictionary.

hyponym

A words is described as a hyponym when it is an exemplification of another word. So 'oak' is a hyponym of 'tree', for example.

informal

Informal language is the kind of language used when speakers or writers feel confident of their audience and relaxed with them. It uses contractions ('isn't' for 'is not') and a range of vocabulary considered unsuitable for formal language (e.g. 'plod', 'filth', or 'cop', instead of 'police officer'). Informal language may also use slightly different grammar (e.g. 'I done it' instead of 'I did it').

loan word

A borrowing: a word that has come into English from another language.

noun

A class of words used to refer to people things and ideas. Most nouns satisfy all or most of the following tests:
they can be preceded by *a, an, or the*
a pen, an answer, the train
they have a singular and a plural form:
one pen, two pens
they can be preceded by an adjective:
blue pens, interesting answers

passive vocabulary

The words that you understand when you see or hear them but which you don't (yet) feel confident to use yourself. So they are passive because you don't actively use them.

prefix

An affix that comes at the beginning of a word. For example: 'pre-', 'inter-', and 'peri-'.

preposition

A class of words. Prepositions are words that are placed before a noun, pronoun, or noun phrase to form a prepositional phrase:
with marbles (noun)
to me (pronoun)
down a long dusty road (noun phrase)
The commonest are:

about	above	across	after	against	along
among	around	as	at	before	behind

pronoun

A class of words. Pronouns are a class of words that 'stand in for' other words, typically for nouns, noun phrases, and other pronouns. They enable the writer or speaker to refer to a word, expression, or idea that has already been mentioned, without having to repeat it. Examples are :
I/me, you, he/him, she/her, etc.
mine, yours, hers, etc.
myself, yourself, etc.
this, that, these, those

readability

A text is readable by someone if the language used means that they are capable of understanding it. The word is also more loosely used to describe a text that the reader thinks is worth making the effort to read. Readability is the measure of how readable a text is.

register

The vocabulary and grammar we use to communicate are determined by the social context (who we are communicating with) and our purpose in communicating. Some situations and purposes have highly specialized registers (e.g. legal contracts and financial journalism).

subordinating conjunction

Conjunctions that link two words or groups of words that are not of equal status in a sentence. One of the two is subordinate to the other. They are often used to link two or more clauses:

Main clause		Subordinate clause
I'll tell you	**when**	I feel like it.

SUBORDINATING CONJUNCTION

Subordinating conjunctions can also link words ('He was dependable *although* boring') and phrases ('She was pleased to be there, *if* worried about the outcome').

suffix

An affix that comes at the end of a word. Suffixes are normally used to turn one base word into another word. So, for example, 'beauty' becomes 'beautify' and 'possess' becomes 'possessive'. '-ify' and '-ive' are suffixes.

taboo

Certain words are considered unacceptable in 'polite society'. The group of words that are taboo changes with time. For example, when Shaw's *Pygmalion* was first produced, London society was shocked (or professed to be) at its use of the word 'bloody'. Today people are rather more difficult to shock, but it is still possible.

thesaurus

A word book in which words are arranged thematically to assist the user in selecting the right word for a specific purpose.

verb

A class of words. Verbs are used:

- to express an action

  She fled.
- to express a state

  She dreamed.
- to link the subject with a later part of the sentence

  She was alone.

Regular verbs have these forms:

Stem: walk

Present tense: walk/walks

Past tense: walked

Present participle: walking

Past participle: walked

Further reading and resources

There are three main types of resource available to those who wish to get a better grip on words:

■ books;

■ computer-based resources;

■ web-based resources.

Books

As was stressed earlier, it is essential to have a reliable dictionary for instant reference. Those of a suitable size for this purpose include:

The Concise Oxford Dictionary
Oxford University Press Revised 2nd Edition 2001, 1,728 pages.

The New Oxford Dictionary of English
Oxford University Press 1999, 2,174 pages.

Collins English Dictionary
HarperCollins 2000, 1,824 pages.

The New Penguin English Dictionary
Penguin 2001, 1,656 pages.

A good thesaurus is also an indispensable tool. My favourite is:

Thesaurus
Bloomsbury 1997, 1,216 pages

Also good are:

The New Oxford Thesaurus of English
Oxford University Press 2000, 1,097 pages

The New Penguin Thesaurus
Penguin 2001, 676 pages

Spelling

In this series there is an excellent book on *Spelling* by Robert Allen.

Grammar

Everyday Grammar by John Seely
Oxford University Press, 2001

Computer-based

I'm probably being old-fashioned, but with two notable exceptions I don't find computer-based reference materials particularly helpful. Those two exceptions are:

- **The Oxford English Dictionary on CD-ROM**
  (2nd edition). If you need the power of a really big dictionary then there is no competitor. And the CD-ROM version is vastly easier to consult than the multi-volume print version. The *OED* is also available by subscription on-line.

- **The Encyclopedia Britannica**
  Available on a CD-ROM for convenience, or free on-line for cheapness.

Having said that, I have to confess to finding the electronic version of the *Concise Oxford,* which sits on your desktop for instant access, very helpful for quick checks on words.

Web-based

As with many things on the web, it's difficult to know where to begin. If you are involved with any kind of writing, then you should consult:

The Internet: A Writer's Guide by Jane Dorner
A&C Black, 2000, 200 pages

and its associated website: www.internetwriter.co.uk, which has an excellent set of links which are updated monthly, at great expense and effort by Jane.

The other new and exciting website to look at is www.askoxford.com, on which you will find, among other things, material linked to this and other books in the series.

Permissions

For permission to quote copyright material I thank: Steven Morgan Friedman for 'Unicarp: Dedicated to Excellence'.

Index

Note: page numbers in **bold** refer to definitions. Example words explained in detail are in *italics*